1,000,000 Books

are available to read at

---◆---

www.ForgottenBooks.com

---◆---

Read online
Download PDF
Purchase in print

ISBN 978-0-259-97333-1
PIBN 10835996

English
Français
Deutsche
Italiano
Español
Português

www.forgottenbooks.com

Mythology Photography **Fiction**
Fishing Christianity **Art** Cooking
Essays Buddhism Freemasonry
Medicine **Biology** Music **Ancient**
Egypt Evolution Carpentry Physics
Dance Geology **Mathematics** Fitness
Shakespeare **Folklore** Yoga Marketing
Confidence Immortality Biographies
Poetry **Psychology** Witchcraft
Electronics Chemistry History **Law**
Accounting **Philosophy** Anthropology
Alchemy Drama Quantum Mechanics
Atheism Sexual Health **Ancient History**
Entrepreneurship Languages Sport
Paleontology Needlework Islam
Metaphysics Investment Archaeology
Parenting Statistics Criminology
Motivational

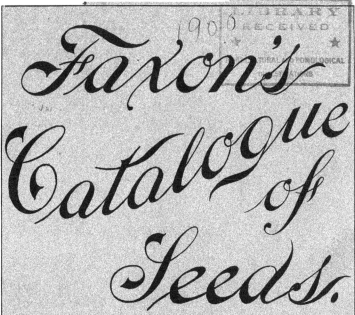

Faxon's Catalogue of Seeds.

To Our Friends and Patrons:

Nothing would give us greater pleasure than to be able to personally thank each and every one of our friends and customers for their generous patronage during the year that is past, but although this is impossible, we can and do most gratefully acknowledge your many favors, and extend to all our best wishes for a happy and prosperous New Year, through the medium of this, Our Annual Seed Catalogue.

STANDARD SEEDS.—We have freed our lists of Vegetables and Flowers from the incumbrance of undesirable sorts; consequently they are much easier to make selections from than longer lists, where poor and worthless varieties are intermingled with the good and valuable. These lists we call **Standard Seeds.**

FAXON'S SPECIALTIES.—Under this head are catalogued those Flowers and Vegetables the cultivation of which we have made a study, and we believe our strains of seed of these varieties will compare favorably with any to be obtained. The flowers referred to are:—ASTERS, PANSIES, SWEET PEAS, AND NASTURTIUMS; the vegetables:—TRUE YELLOW GLOBE DANVERS ONION, SAVOY CABBAGE, CAULIFLOWER, AND DANVERS CARROT. These sorts you will find catalogued on the succeeding pages, and distinctly marked

FAXON'S SPECIALTIES.

NURSERY STOCK AND PLANTS.—This branch of our business is giving the greatest satisfaction to our customers—for the reason, that having our own Nursery and Greenhouses we can and do personally select each customer's order. Our stock of Roses, Shade Trees, Ornamental Shrubs, Fruit Trees, Small Fruits and Bedding Plants is very complete and of the best quality. We know that our nursery stock, plants and bulbs will prove most reliable in every respect.

REMITTANCES.—Remittances should be made by post-office money order, bank draft, the cash by registered letter, or express order. For fractional parts of a dollar, postage stamps will be received, two-cent denominations preferred.

SEEDS BY MAIL.—Seeds by the packet or ounce, either Flower or Vegetable Seeds, will be sent by mail at catalogue prices without extra charge. Seeds at pound and quart prices we do not send free; kindly add eight cents per pound, or ten cents per quart on Corn, and sixteen cents per quart on Beans and Peas to catalogue prices.

SEEDS BY EXPRESS OR FREIGHT.—No charge is made for delivery to Freight Depots or Express Offices in Boston—forwarding charges to be borne by the purchaser.

BAGS USED IN PACKING ORDERS are furnished as follows:—One-quarter bushel, ten cents; one-half bushel, fifteen cents; one bushel, twenty cents; two bushels, twenty-five cents. No charge for boxes or barrels.

ORDER SHEET AND RETURN ENVELOPE.—Kindly use the enclosed order sheet for writing out your orders; fill in your full name and address, amount sent, etc., as per blanks, and mail to us in the printed return envelope enclosed; by so doing there is no danger of orders being lost in the mails.

SEASON OF 1900.

M. B. Faxon
Boston, Mass.

31 STATE STREET,

A STANDARD VEGETABLE.

THE FAXON SQUASH

A distinctive feature of this squash is that the ripe squashes vary in color, some of them being pale yellow with still paler yellow stripes in hollows, while others are green, mottled, and faintly striped with a lighter green. In this respect it is different from all other varieties, and after years of careful trial we have found that this squash follows its type absolutely true, and we can offer this squash to you as a distinct new vegetable.

☞ WE HAVE SPENT YEARS IN PERFECTING THE FAXON SQUASH, AND WE NOW ASK YOU TO GIVE OUR NEW VEGETABLE A TRIAL. The flesh is a deep orange yellow, cavity very small, and seeds few; the special peculiarity, however, is that, while uncooked it appears to have a shell like any squash, when cooked there is practically none, the shell or inedible part being only about as thick as a sheet of writing paper. It is the best squash we ever tasted—sweet and very dry—and for squash pies it must be tried to be appreciated. We know a trial will convince all of its great value.

It matures early and can be used as a summer squash. It is the best winter variety we know of, being a very late keeper, we having repeatedly had squashes in our cellar in perfect condition in April and May. It is the only squash we ever saw that every specimen is of superior quality without regard to size or whether it is ripe or green. This is a very desirable feature, as many squashes (the Hubbard especially) must be thoroughly ripe before frost, or the crop is lost. It is not so with "The Faxon Squash"; every specimen can be gathered and used.

Very early, enormously productive, of medium size and the best possible quality, we fully believe that this new variety is destined to become a standard amongst squashes, both for home use and market purposes.

After most carefully testing this new squash for ten years, and having had many of the very best squash experts in this country thoroughly try this vegetable for the same period—the universal verdict is that "THE FAXON SQUASH" is by far the best squash in cultivation for the kitchen garden.

Per Liberal Packet 5 cents; 6 Packets for 25 cents; Ounce 10 cents; ¼ Pound 30 cents; Pound $1.00. By mail, postage paid.

OUR ANNUAL INTRODUCTION OFFER.

SEASON OF 1900.

Feeling confident that a trial of our seeds will make a regular customer of the most critical buyer, and also to show our appreciation of the many orders our friends have sent us in the past, we again make the following special offer:

☞ With every order (accompanied by the cash) for One Dollar's worth or more of seeds in packets or ounces, selected from this "Catalogue," we will send without charge, one packet of

FAXON'S "WHITE HOUSE" PANSIES,

price of which alone is 50 cents

In order to obtain this packet of Pansy Seed without charge, the following conditions must be strictly followed.

1. The order sent must be for one dollar's worth or more of seeds in packets or ounces.
2. The cash must accompany the order.
3. The enclosed Coupon must accompany the order.

☞ OUR ANNUAL INTRODUCTION OFFER is in addition, to all other special offers in this catalogue that refer to Packets and Ounces. ☜

COUPON.

This Coupon is good for one packet of

Faxon's "White House" Pansies

when accompanied with an order for One Dollar's worth or more of Seeds in packets or ounces, as explained on preceding page.

Season of 1900.

31 STATE STREET.

M. B. Faxon
Boston Mass.

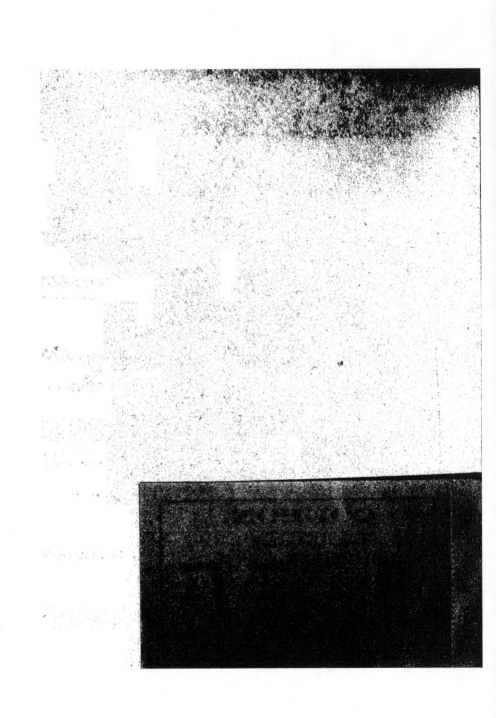

FAXON'S "WHITE HOUSE" PANSIES.

FAXON'S
SPECIALTIES

Packet 50 cents.
5 Packets for $2.00.
Trade Packet $1.00.
6 Trade Packets for $5.00.
Ounce $15.00.

FAXON'S "WHITE HOUSE" PANSIES—*Engraved from a Photograph.*

After almost twenty years of painstaking care; I am able to offer you, what I believe to be the richest and most magnificent collection of pansies ever produced in this country. The individual flowers are very large, frequently measuring three to four inches in diameter; while the plants themselves are strong and robust. My mixture is noted for freedom of bloom, brilliancy of coloring, perfection of form, and splendid substance.

This is the Finest Mixture I have ever been able to produce.

Price, per packet, 50 cents; 5 packets for $2.00.   Trade packet, for florists and those who wish larger quantity, $1.00; 6 trade packets for $5.00. Ounce $15.00.

HOW TO GROW PANSIES. In regard to the cultivation of the pansy, I usually begin making plantings of the seed early in February, and continue at intervals through the season. The young plants are treated the same as described for asters, and are transplanted into beds in the garden as soon as the ground becomes dry and warm. Set the plants at least one foot apart each way, more space is better than less, and water thoroughly in dry weather. Pick off the buds as soon as they appear, during the summer months, which will cause the plants to grow bushy and compact, and bloom profusely during the late autumn and early spring months. For late or early spring flowering, sow the seed in August, and plant out into beds in October. Cover the plants during the winter with evergreen boughs or other coarse material. The pansy delights in a deep, moist, cool soil, enriched with plenty of well-decayed cow manure; a partially shaded situation is best for pansies. They will not do well under trees, but in some location where the sun strikes only part of each day the most satisfactory results can be obtained.

It is now more than twenty years that I have made a study of the cultivation of Asters — during that time I have grown, both for the market and exhibition purposes, all classes and varieties, as well as all novelties in this flower introduced from time to time both by foreign and American seedsmen — and every season my opinion has strengthened that three classes of asters practically include the cream of the list; these three asters are Truffaut's Pæony-Flowered Perfection, the Victoria, and the Imbricated Pompon. Truffaut's Pæony-Flowered Perfection and the Victoria are both large asters; the petals of the former incurving to the centre, the petals of the latter recurving to the edge (see illustration). Imbricated Pompon Asters have small flowers about the size of a half-dollar. No garden is complete without its bed of asters, and if some of each variety above noted is planted, I feel sure your asters cannot be anything but a grand success.

Through my long acquaintance with the growers of aster seed all over the world, together with my own experience; I cannot but feel that my strains of seed of these flowers will compare most favorably with any to be obtained. I am not offering you novelties; on the contrary, these flowers are old garden favorites, that with years of care and study have been grown to perfection.

Below you will find listed my **Best Asters**, and on the next page full descriptions of the three splendid classes, a blending of which seed composes :—

Faxon's Royal Mixed Asters.

This strain is the *ne plus ultra* of all varieties, and is composed of the three magnificent classes described on the next page. No aster seed that has ever been sent out will give better results than this superb mixture of Truffaut's Pæony-Flowered Perfection, the Victoria and the Imbricated Pompon varieties. Every packet contains over thirty distinct shades of color. This seed represents the highest perfection in asters, and for private gardens is unsurpassed, giving a great variety for a little money.

FAXON'S ROYAL MIXED ASTER SEED.
Price Per Large Packet, 25 Cents; 5 Large Packets for $1.00; Ounce, $5.00.

TRUFFAUT'S PÆONY-FLOWERED PERFECTION ASTERS

This elegant aster shares with the "Victoria" the distinction of being, to my mind, the best of the whole family. **The individual flowers are large and especially prized for their brightness of color.** Perfectly double, with each petal distinctly incurving to the centre, as shown by the illustration on preceding page the left-hand flower). This variety attains a height of from eighteen inches to two feet and the entire plant makes a perfect mass of bloom. For the very best results a rich, loamy soil should be selected for your aster bed, and as the roots of the plants are produced near the surface, a mulching of rotten manure will be found most beneficial. "**My Splendid Mixture**" embraces about thirty distinct shades of color, from the purest white to the very darkest purple; and is the best that I have ever been able to offer.

Price, Per Large Packet, 25 Cents ; 5 Large Packets For $1.00 ; Ounce, $5.00.

VICTORIA ASTERS.

Many amateur and professional gardeners contend that this is the finest aster in cultivation; but be that as it may, it is certainly an elegant variety. **The blooms are most beautiful and perfectly-formed, and besides the great value of this sort as a garden plant, it is also the very best of all asters for pot-culture.** They can be grown and flowered wholly in pots if desired. This aster is also a large-flowered variety, and like the preceding grows from one and one-half to two feet in height; but the petals, instead of incurving to the centre, recurve to the edge of the flower; giving a most beautiful effect — see the illustration on opposite page **(the right-hand flower). The "Victoria," and "Truffaut's Pæony-Flowered Perfection," varieties are the very best of all for exhibition purposes ;** producing as they do the finest and largest flowers of the brightest and most exquisite shades and colors. "**My Splendid Mixture**" of Victoria Aster Seed is unrivalled and contains every desirable color yet produced.

Price, Per Large Packet, 25 Cents ; 5 Large Packets For $1.00 ; Ounce, $5.00.

Boston Florists' Double White Asters.

This aster, which is a selected strain of the purest white "Victoria Aster," is by all growers admitted to be the very best of all white varieties; and is especially valuable to Florists, and for all purposes where pure white flowers are desired. **For many years the Florists near Boston, Mass., have given great care and attention to the improvement and culture of this variety, until the greatest perfection has been attained.** The seed which I am able to offer you is saved only from the most perfectly double flowers and is of the very purest white. This is the very best white aster for cut-flowers, and is largely used by both florists and private growers.

Price, Per Packet, 15 Cents ; 8 Packets For $1.00 ; Ounce, $4.00.

IMBRICATED POMPON ASTERS.

This class is unquestionably the best of the small-flowered sorts. **Each plant forms a most perfect mass of bloom ; in fact every plant might well be called a perfect bouquet in itself.** This aster grows about twenty inches in height, and there are many very beautiful colors in this class. For exhibition purposes it is very desirable — when in full bl om the whole plant is usually cut and placed in a vase and it is easy to picture the grand effect a stand of these asters will produce; there being over twenty splendid colors and shades.

Splendid Mixture. Price, Per Large Packet, 25 Cents ; 5 Large Packets For $1.00 ; Ounce, $5.00.

HOW TO GROW ASTERS. I commence making plantings of the seed in February, and continue every ten days or two weeks until into June, in order that I may have flowers throughout the season. For the best results the seed should be sown in shallow boxes, in the greenhouse or sunny window; cover lightly with fine soil, and keep moderately moist until the plants are well up, then transplant into small pots, or set the plants three inches apart in shallow boxes. This will give you good stocky plants that will immediately start a strong growth when planted in the garden. As soon as the weather is warm and settled the plants should be set in the open ground, in rows or in beds, as the cultivator may prefer, but in either case the plants should be set at least one foot apart each way. If the weather is dry when the plants are set out, they must be watered until they become thoroughly established in their new position. Keep the soil loose and free from weeds, and when the plants are about two thirds grown, they should be tied up to stakes. A rich, loamy soil is the best for asters, and as the roots are produced near the surface, a mulching of rotten manure is very beneficial. I earnestly advise all to plant generously of these magnificent annuals.

3

Faxon's BEST Mixed-Sweet Peas.

FAXON'S
BOSTON MIXTURE
SWEET PEAS

C.S.COBURN CO.
SC.

SWEET PEAS. FAXON'S SPECIALTIES.

Faxon's "Boston Mixture."

A leading American seedsman has called the sweet pea "Fashion's Fragrant, Favorite Flower,"—a most excellent description; for certainly the sweet pea for garden decoration, corsage bouquets. and all purposes for which cut-flowers are employed, is everywhere appreciated. **I wish to place particular stress upon the fact that my mixture of sweet peas is composed exclusively of the improved large-flowering varieties. Only the very newest and most desirable colors and shades are included; which have been especially selected for their graceful form, superb coloring, and delicious fragrance.**

When, twelve years ago (August 14, 1886), The Massachusetts Horticultural Society awarded me a First-Class Certificate of Merit for Sweet Peas, I thought that my collection of this beautiful and fragrant hardy annual was nearly complete. Then I had about twenty sorts ; today I have more than one hundred distinct named varieties; but it is not alone in this remarkable increase of named kinds that has given the sweet pea the position it now holds, but also in the extraordinary and wonderful advance that has been made in the size of the individual flowers. Besides, many entirely new and exquisitely delicate shades have recently been introduced, accompanied by a most marked increase in the free-blooming habit of the plant.

Faxon's "Boston Mixture" Sweet Peas

Contains more than one hundred distinct named varieties in splendid mixture.

PRICE, PER PACKET 5 CTS.; 15 CTS. PER OUNCE; 50 CTS. PER 1-4 POUND; $1.50 PER POUND.

HOW TO GROW SWEET PEAS. It is now universally conceded that the sweet pea is one of the most desirable annuals in cultivation. Its delicate fragrance, beautiful form, and variety of coloring, make it a favorite with the florist; while its easy culture and long continuance of blooming make secure its cultivation in every flower garden. The seed should be sown in drills, and covered at least six inches deep. This may be done in two ways. Having prepared the ground and made the drills of the desired depth, we may drop the seed and draw into the drill earth enough to cover the seed two inches deep; as soon as the plants appear through this covering draw into the drill two inches more earth; and so on until the drill has been filled up even with the surface of the ground. Or, secondly, the seed may be dropped and covered in the usual manner, at a single operation. The surface of the ground sometimes becomes dry and hard just as the young plants are about to appear; especially so after a shower followed by a hot sun. Unless some means is taken to prevent this, a great many of the young plants will fail to break through the soil, and those annoying "gaps" will appear in the rows. A slight raking just as the plants are breaking ground will prevent this, and also kill any small weeds that may have started. Sweet Peas should be bushed almost as soon as they are well up. Birch brush, the same as we use for tall growing garden peas, is good for this purpose. Wire hen netting makes a very desirable trellis for them to run upon, and is very neat. Whatever they are trained upon must be very firmly secured in position, so that the vines, when fully grown, will not be blown down. Sweet Peas are very easily grown and, if the above directions for their culture are followed, I think no one will fail to have success with this favorite flower. But before leaving this subject, let me state what I believe to be the keynote of successful sweet pea culture, which, in nine seasons out of ten, will give success; it is short and easily remembered:—**Plant Deep.** As regards the selection of seed for planting, I have as a rule found that a choice mixture of colors gives the best satisfaction, and have always taken the greatest pains to have my mixture contain all the desirable sorts in cultivation, both new and old. This year my mixture is far better than ever before, and I feel confident that you will be amply repaid by planting my strain.

FAXON'S NASTURTIUMS

FAXON'S SPECIALTIES.

These beautiful bedding and climbing plants flower most profusely, and remain in full bloom a long time even when planted in the poorest soil. I have kept my collection up to the very highest standard, and I am convinced that no better seed can be obtained. My mixtures include all the most rare and beautiful colors, from the very lightest shades of yellow and white to the rich, dark velvety colors so much prized. **On the next page you will find the different kinds fully described.** By planting some of each sort your garden will be a most gorgeous sight all summer. Every one should grow some of my Nasturtiums.

HOW TO GROW NASTURTIUMS.

The ease with which Nasturtiums can be grown has always made them a great favorite everywhere, and it has always impressed me that, as a rule, this flower attains greater perfection in the average garden than almost any other annual. It is of the easiest culture, and will flourish in any good garden soil. Simply take pains as you would with any other flower to thoroughly loosen the soil before the seeds are planted. Scatter the seeds thinly in rows or beds, and cover about one and one half inches deep with fine soil, pressing the soil down firmly. When well up, thin to not less than six inches apart so that the plants may have plenty of room in which to grow. From now until the flowers begin to form, cultivate often; but as soon as the buds begin to show color, stop all further stirring of the soil, and disturb as little as possible. To have Nasturtiums in full bloom until the frost comes, it is necessary to keep the blossoms well picked off, and on no account ever allowing flowers to wither on the vines, as that will put a stop to their blooming. If every morning you pick off every flower that is fully expanded, or seems in the least withered, you will be surprised at the beautiful bed of flowers that will be the result. Of course judgment must be used in this matter. We have only tried to explain results in a general way, and we will here say that this same method of keeping flowers in bloom applies to all annuals, especially to Sweet Peas.

Faxon's Champion Nasturtiums.

☞ My Nasturtiums,—during the past fifteen years,—have been awarded; many "First Prizes" at the Massachusetts Horticultural Society's Shows and elsewhere; and I know, that for rich and brilliant colors as well as great variety, that my various mixtures are unsurpassed.

FAXON'S CHAMPION TALL NASTURTIUMS.

This is my own strain of the well-known tall or climbing variety, the most beautiful and luxuriant annual that can be used for covering trellises, arbors, or rustic work; of the easiest culture, bearing its gorgeous flowers in elegant profusion until killed by the frost.

FINEST MIXED COLORS.

Per packet, 5 cents; 15 cents per ounce; 50 cents per ¼ pound; $1.50 per pound.

FAXON'S CHAMPION DWARF NASTURTIUMS.

My special mixture of this most showy and popular annual is noted for its great variety of rich colored flowers. The plants grow about one foot in height, and being of very compact habit, are much used for bedding. Dwarf Nasturtiums thrive under all weathers and conditions, and making gorgeous masses of color through the entire summer are unsurpassed for garden decoration.

FINEST MIXED COLORS.

Per packet, 5 cents; 25 cents per ounce; 75 cents per ¼ pound; $2.50 per pound.

FAXON'S "TROPÆOLUM LOBBIANUM" VARIETIES.

This is a running species (Lobb's Nasturtiums), with leaves and flowers somewhat smaller than the above varieties; but their greater profusion renders them superb for hanging vases, arbor and rock-work. The flowers are of the most rich and brilliant colors. This variety is also much cultivated for window decoration in the window garden and conservatory.

FINEST MIXED COLORS.

Per packet, 10 cents; 40 cents per ounce; $1.25 per ¼ pound; $4.50 per pound.

A GREAT SPECIAL SALE OF TWO ELEGANT HARDY SHRUBS.

The Hardy Garden Hydrangea.

(*Hydrangea Paniculata Grandiflora.*)

Recognizing the sterling worth of this grandest of all hardy flowering Shrubs, we have for many years past made it a leading specialty, **and it is to-day the most popular of all Shrubs for yard, lawn and cemetery planting**; it is extensively used for hedge planting and for clumps and screens. The great reduction now made in the prices should still further its popularity. It readily attains a height of 5 to 7 feet; hardy in all localities, and needs no protection in Winter; blooms the first and every season in July and August, when other flowers are scarce, and continues in bloom for two or three months; the flowers are massive, cone shaped, often measuring ten inches in length, and have a pleasing variation of color, changing from the original pure white to pink, and finally a beautiful rich coppery red. When the flowers mature they can be cut and utilized as parlor ornaments, where they retain their natural beauty for an indefinite time. Our engraving, reproduced from a photograph of a single plant growing on our grounds, does not exaggerate in the slightest degree the flowering propensities of **Hydrangea Paniculata Grandiflora.** All our plants will give a like result, and cannot fail to prove a source of genuine pleasure and admiration.

LARGE, EXTRA-STRONG PLANTS 50 cts. each; 5 for $2.50; 10 for $4.50; 50 for $20; $35 per 100.

☛ I deliver all Nursery Stock securely and properly packed to the express office or freight depot in Boston, as the customer may prefer — forwarding charges to be borne by the purchaser.

New Double White Japan Snowball.

This grand New Double White Japan Snowball is undoubtedly the king of all hardy flowering Shrubs. Do not confuse it with the common Snowball which does not approach it in any particular; it blooms in June, **when the whole bush is completely covered and loaded down with great compact balls of pure white double flowers, like miniature Roses.** These magnificent balls of flowers are borne in such great profusion that they almost completely hide the leaves and branches, and the whole bush appears one dense mass of bloom; the tree is of erect bushy growth, with deep glossy green leaves having a peculiar crimped and crinkled appearance; grows 6 to 8 feet high, and is entirely hardy, needing no protection of any kind. The immense stock we now have is the result of many years of careful work. Our fine illustration, which, though not nearly as handsome as the plant itself, gives some idea of its wonderful beauty. We can cordially recommend it as one of the very best Hardy Ornamental Flowering Shrubs for dooryard, lawn and park planting; it is also very suitable for cemeteries, as it is vigorous and hardy, and sure to bloom, and being quite scarce and rare, it always attracts a great deal of attention wherever seen. It is one of the things you don't want to miss getting, and ours is the true genuine variety, propagated from large old blooming plants here on our own grounds. Note the reduced prices.

EXTRA-STRONG, LARGE PLANTS

50 cts. each;
5 for $2.50;
10 for $4.50;
50 for $20;
$35 per 100.

☛ I deliver all Nursery Stock securely and properly packed to the express office or freight depot in Boston, as the customer may prefer — forwarding charges to be borne by the purchaser.

VIBURNUM PLICATUM.

NEW DOUBLE WHITE JAPAN SNOWBALL.

8

HARDY ROSES.

HYBRID PERPETUAL ROSES are perfectly hardy, and very free bloomers, and are unquestionably the most desirable variety for the garden. We have added many new sorts, and our collection now includes the choicest kinds. A rich soil is essential in growing roses, and it is well to apply a heavy dressing of manure to the beds in the fall. In the spring the bushes should be well cut back. The plants offered are the very largest and best, and will immediately make fine blooming bushes. We can supply smaller plants when desired.

Dormant plants, 50 cts. each; $4.00 per dozen.

In regard to sorts, we can, as a rule, give a better selection when the choice of kinds is left to us; kindly specify what colors you prefer. (These plants are too large for mailing, and should be sent by express.)

HARDY MOSS ROSES—50 cts. each; $4.00 per doz.
HARDY CLIMBING ROSES—50 cts. each; $4.00 per dozen.
EVER-BLOOMING TEA ROSES—Splendid assortment for the summer garden. $1.50 to $3.00 per doz.

HARDY ORNAMENTAL SHRUBS.

☞ The prices quoted are for selected single specimens ; special rates by the dozen and hundred on application.

ALMOND—Double Pink-Flowering. 50 cts.
   Double White-Flowering. 50 cts.
ALTHEA—Purple, Red or White. Each 50 cts.
AZALEAS—The best varieties. $1.00 to $3.00.
BERBERIS THUNBERGII—The best Barberry. 50 cts.
CALYCANTHUS FLORIDUS—(Spice Bush). 50 cts.
CHIONANTHUS VIRGINICA—(White Fringe). 50 cts. to $1.00.
CORNUS FLORIDA—(Dogwood), White. 50 cts.
   Red. $1.00.
CYDONIA JAPONICA—(Japan Quince). 50 cts.
CYTISUS LABURNUM—(Golden Chain). $1.00.
DEUTZIA—Crenata, Double white. 50 cts.
   Crenata, Double pink. 50 cts.
   Gracilis, Pure white. 50 cts.
EUONYMUS—(Strawberry-Bush). 50 cts.
EXOCHORDA GRANDIFLORA—White. 50 cts. to $1.00.
FORSYTHIA SUSPENSA—Yellow. 50 cts.
HAWTHORN—Paul's Scarlet. $1.50.
   Double White. $1.50.
LILACS—White. 50 cts.
   Purple. 50 cts.
MAGNOLIAS—Best varieties. $1.00 to $3.00.
MOUNTAIN LAUREL—(Kalmia). 50 cts.
PRIVET—Golden-Leaved. 50 cts.
   California. 50 cts.
PRUNUS PISSARDI—(Purple-Leaved Plum). 50 cts.
   Triloba (Double pink). 50 cts.
PYRUS MALUS PARKMANNI—Beautiful. $1.00.
RHODODENDRONS—Hardiest Hybrids. $1.00 to $3.00.
SAMBUGUS AUREA—(Golden Elder). 50 cts.
SPIRÆAS—Prunifolia, Double white. 50 cts.
   Thunbergii ; white, beautiful. 50 cts.
   Van Houttei ; white, splendid. 50 cts.
   Anthony Waterer, rose-color. 75 cts.
SYRINGA—Golden. 50 cts.
   Sweet-Scented, white. 50 cts.
SNOWBERRY—Pink, with white berries. 50 cts.
WEIGELIA—Pure White. 50 cts.
   Beautiful rose-color. 50 cts.
   Pink with variegated foliage. 50 cts.
YUCCA FILAMENTOSA—(Adam's Needle). 50 cts.

EVERGREEN TREES AND SHRUBS.

☞ The prices quoted are for selected single specimens ; special rates by the dozen and hundred on application.

ARBOR VITÆ. 25 cts. to $1.00.
FIR—(Balsam). 50 cts. to $1.00.
JUNIPER. 50 cts. to $1.50.
PINE—25 cts. to $1.50.
SPRUCE—Norway. 50 cts. to $1.50.
   Hemlock. 25 cts. to $1.00.
   Colorado Blue. $2.50 to $5.00.

HARDY HEDGE PLANTS.

☞ Special rates quoted for large quantities on application.

ARBOR VITÆ—1 ft. ; doz. $1.00 ; hundred, $6.00.
BARBERRY—2 ft. ; doz. $2.00 ; hundred, $15.00.
JAPAN QUINCE—1 ft. ; doz. $1.75 ; hundred, $12.00.
PRIVET—California. 2½ ft. ; doz. $2.00 ; hundred, $15.00.
RUSSIAN MULBERRY—2 ft. ; doz., $2.00 ; hundred, $15.00.

ORNAMENTAL AND SHADE TREES.

☞ The prices quoted are for selected single specimens ; special rates by the dozen and hundred on application.

ASH—American White. 75 cts. to $1.00.
   Cut-Leaved. $1.50 to $2.00.
   Mountain. $1.00 to $1.50.
BEECH—American. 75 cts. to $1.00.
   River's Purple. $1.00 to $5.00.
BIRCH—White. 75 cts. to $1.50.
   Cut-Leaved, Weeping. $1.00 to $3.00.
CATALPA—Speciosa. 50 cts. to $1.50.
ELM—American. 50 cts. to $1.50.
   English. 50 cts. to $1.50.
HORSE-CHESTNUT—White-Flowering. $1.00 to $2.00.
   Red-Flowering. $1.00 to $2.50.
SWEET-CHESTNUT—75 cts. to $1.50.
LARCH—European. 75 cts. to $1.50.
LINDEN—(Basswood). 75 cts. to $2.00.
LOCUST—75 cts. to $1.50.
MAPLE—Sugar or Rock. 50 cts. to $2.00.
   Norway. $1.00 to $2.00.
   Silver. 50 cts. to $1.50.
   Japanese. $2.00 to $3.00.
   Weir's Cut-Leaved. $1.00 to $2.50.
OAK—White. 50 cts. to $1.00.
   English. 75 cts. to $1.50.
POPLAR—Lombardy. 50 cts. to $2.00.
WILLOW—Kilmarnock. 75 cts. to $2.00.

HARDY CLIMBING PLANTS.

☞ The prices quoted are for selected single specimens ; special rates by the dozen and hundred on application.

ACTINIDIA POLYGAMA—50 cts. to $1.00.
AMPELOPSIS VEITCHII—25 cts. to $1.00.
CLEMATIS—Paniculata—Beautiful white. 50 cts. to $1.00.
   Jackmanni—Best purple. 50 cts. to $1.00.
DUTCHMAN'S PIPE—50 cts. to $1.00.
ROXBURY WAX-WORK—50 cts. to $1.00.
HONEYSUCKLE—Hall's Japan. 50 cts. to $1.00.
HOP VINE—35 cts. to 75 cts.
WISTARIA—White or Purple. 50 cts. to $1.00.

FRUIT TREES.

☞ The prices quoted are for selected single specimens ; special rates by the dozen and hundred on application.

APPLES—Early Harvest—Red Astrachan—Sweet Bough—William's Favorite—Gravenstein—Porter—Baldwin—Snow—Hubbardston Nonsuch—Roxbury Russet—King—R. I. Greening—Northern Spy. 50 cts. to $1.00.
CRAB-APPLES—Hyslop—Red Siberian—Transcendent. 50 cts. to $1.00.
CHERRIES—Black Eagle—Black Heart—Black Tartarian—Coe's Transparent—Downer's Late—Governor Wood—Early Richmond. 75 cts. to $1.00.
PEACHES—Crawford's Early—Crawford's Late—Foster—Champion—Crosby. 25 cts. to 75 cts.
PEARS—Bartlett—Clapp's Favorite—Beurre Bosc—Louis Bonne—Seckel—Sheldon—Beurre de Anjou—Dana's Hovey—Lawrence—Winter Nelis. 75 cts. to $1.50.
PLUMS—Bradshaw—Coe's Golden Drop—Green Gage—Jefferson—Lombard. 75 cts. to $1.50.
QUINCES—Orange—Champion. 50 cts. to $1.00.

SMALL FRUITS.

☞ Special rates for large quantities quoted on application.

BLACKBERRIES—Erie—Synder—Dorchester—Wachusett. $1.00 dozen.
CURRANTS—Black Naples—Red Cherry—Fay's Prolific—(Best red variety)—White Dutch—Red Versailles. $1.00 to $2.00 dozen.
DEWBERRY—Lucretia. $1.00 dozen.
GOOSEBERRIES—Downing—Houghton—Industry. $1.50 to $2.50 dozen.
HARDY GRAPES—Concord—Brighton—Delaware—Hartford—Moore's Early—Worden—Moore's Diamond—Niagara—Green Mountain. 25 cts. to 50 cts. each.
NEW HARDY GRAPE—Campbell's Early. $1.00 to $2.00 each.
GRAPES FOR UNDER GLASS—Best Varieties. $1.00 to $2.00 each.
RASPBERRIES—Cuthbert—Marlboro—Gregg. $1.00 dozen.
STRAWBERRIES—Belmont—Bubach—Charles Downing—Sharpless—Gandy—Marshall. Layer plants in spring, $1.00 per hundred; pot-grown plants after August 1st, $2.50 per hundred.

Faxon's "Massachusetts Prize" Hollyhocks.

No garden should be without its bed of hollyhocks, and considering the magnificent varieties which have recently been introduced, it is not surprising that this grand old flower should have again come into popular favor. To my mind what makes the hollyhock so

SPIKES OF "MASSACHUSETTS PRIZE" HOLLYHOCKS.

valuable as a garden plant, is its hardiness—for when once well established it will continue for years to bloom more bountifully each succeeding season. Great, large, double blossoms can now be had from almost black to the purest white, together with all the other splendid and superbly brilliant colors.

It has been a labor of many years to get together my present collection; some of my very best varieties I have obtained from other seedsmen, and I have also secured many very beautiful sorts from private growers. You can raise your own hollyhocks from the seed or purchase the plants as you prefer. I grow annually a large number of plants and if you wish immediate effect I would advise you to purchase them—but you will have no trouble in raising your hollyhocks from the seed. **Never since I have been growing hollyhocks, has my collection equalled its present effectiveness, both as regards variety of colors and perfect doubleness of bloom. Our trial grounds this past season were simply gorgeous with blooming hollyhocks from July until the frost came. My strain is a mixture of every conceivable shade and color, and the seed is saved from the very choicest double flowers.**

Faxon's "Massachusetts Prize" Hollyhocks.

MY VERY CHOICEST DOUBLE MIXED SEED.

PACKET 15 CTS.; 2 PACKETS FOR 25 CTS.
10 PACKETS FOR $1.00; OUNCE $3.00.

PRICES FOR PLANTS. I also offer large, well-grown plants, suitable for immediate blooming at
$2.00 PER DOZEN;
$12.00 PER HUNDRED.

☞ Hollyhock Plants I deliver securely and properly packed to the express office or freight depot in Boston as the customer may prefer—forwarding charges to be borne by the purchaser.

HOW TO GROW HOLLYHOCKS.

Hollyhocks succeed nicely in almost any good garden soil that is well drained and thoroughly manured. The seed is sown either in the spring or late summer. In the spring the seed is sown in pots or shallow boxes, and the young plants cared for the same as recommended for asters. In July or August the seed can be planted directly in a nicely prepared bed in the garden, and good plants be obtained for the next season's blooming. For the best results the young plants should be transplanted several times before being placed in the beds where they are permanently to remain. A stiff stake will be requisite for each plant, and it should be placed in position before injury is caused by rough wind. After the flowering season is over, the plants should be cut down to about eight inches from the ground, and at the approach of cold weather well protected for the winter with plenty of strawy manure or other coarse material.

10

The Boston POPPIES.

THE BOSTON POPPIES·

The recent wonderful development of these old-fashioned flowers has brought them into great and deserved popularity; this is not strange when we stop and consider how many beautiful new varieties have been introduced during the past few years, with the result that we now have a very great number of most desirable kinds from which to make a selection. I think I may safely affirm that no flowers in our gardens afford a more imposing display of brilliant coloring during the blooming season. **The Boston Poppies are a superb mixture of all the best annual varieties, are of quick growth, and also remarkable for their early and free-flowering habit — being gorgeously brilliant throughout June and July.**

Recall to mind every color you have ever seen in Poppies, then imagine every conceivable combination of colors — striped, blotched, edged, and bordered — on both single, semi-double, and double flowers, and you will have but a faint idea of the wondrously varied beauty of The Boston Poppies. **No sight the past summer excited more attention nor called forth more expressions of wonder and amazement than our large block of these Poppies, — with thousands of open flowers of which seemingly there were no two alike.**

Their brilliant, dazzling colorings and wonderful variety make a very effective display in the garden or for cut flowers. As the seed is very small it should be sown quite thinly, and barely covered with the soil. **The Boston Poppies are most easily cultivated, growing very luxuriantly in any situation.**

Seed of THE BOSTON POPPIES.

Price, Per Large Packet, 10 Cents ; 3 Packets for 25 Cents ; 10 Packets for 75 Cents; 1-4 Ounce, 25 Cents ; Ounce, 75 Cents.

NEW GRAND IMPERIAL

JAPANESE MORNING GLORIES

Gigantic Flowers, Exquisite New Colors, Magnificent Foliage.

It is a long time since the introduction of any flower has created the sensation that The New Grand Imperial Japanese Morning Glory has. Few flower-lovers are aware of the wonderful developments that have been made in this flower by those patient and fanciful gardeners, the Japanese. The surpassing charm of these New Grand Imperial Japanese Morning Glories lies in the entrancing beauty and gigantic size of the flowers; they measure from four to six inches across, and their greater substance causes them to remain open much longer than ordinary Morning Glories. **The colors of the flowers, shadings and markings are limitless, and are really wonders of nature, of such incomparable beauty that descriptions are inadequate. Wherever climbers can be grown these should have a prominent place.** Some flowers are of deep, rich velvety tones, others more daintily tinted and shaded than an artist's brush could portray. The solid colors range through reds from soft rose to crimson, bronze and garnet maroon; from daintiest light blue to ultramarine indigo and blackish purple; from snow white to cream and silver gray; some are striped, starred and spotted; others have magnificent edges and throats. The double-flowering sorts are superb and must be seen to be appreciated to their full value. I have tried to write about them as they really are; but words will not describe the wondrous beauty of the flowers. Perhaps the following description, taken from the catalogue of one of the largest growers of the seed, will prove not only interesting to you, but may give you a true idea of just what The New Grand Imperial Japanese Morning Glories are.

"To begin to describe the colors, shadings, hues, combinations of colors, variations in markings, would be impossible. Indeed, the beauty and variations are indescribable, and can only be appreciated when seen. One vine will bear blossoms so different that it would seem impossible. As to size and markings of blooms my seed will produce, I will simply say that none of the colored plates in seedsmen's catalogues, that I have ever seen, begins to equal them."

"The foliage also varies in shape, as well as color, latter being from dark green through all shades of green to light yellow, some being variegated with whitish and yellowish green on darker ground. My stock seed was selected by going in person and gathering 10 to 15 seeds from each of the thousands of vines and mixing the whole. This will, I believe, give me the best stock and largest variation in shapes, hues and colors that the world can now show; and superior to any one stock grown anywhere; for the thousands of vines growing together must have hybridized and will cause all the more curious and freakish markings besides bringing forth still more innumerable shades of color."

New Grand Imperial JAPANESE MORNING GLORY SEED.

Superb Mixture. My special mixture of all the very best double and single flowering sorts — a grand assortment. Price, Per Large Packet, 15 Cents; 2 Packets for 25 Cents; 10 Packets for $1.00; Ounce, $1.00.

12

Faxon's Improved Sweet Mignonette

Sweet Mignonette needs no introduction; it is a universal favorite; of the easiest culture, doing equally well in the garden, greenhouse or window box. It grows most rapidly and produces the finest and largest spikes of bloom during the cool, moist weather of the spring and fall months; and can be grown easily in a cool room in winter, if seed is sown in pots early in the fall. The flowers are richer in fragrance when grown in light, sandy soils, but the plants do not grow as vigorously nor are the spikes of bloom as large as when grown in rich, heavy soils. If it is desired to transplant the young seedlings, it should be done when they are quite small, the weather cool and cloudy, and the ground quite moist. **Faxon's Improved Sweet Mignonette is splendid; being deliciously fragrant, and producing the very largest and handsomest spikes of flowers.** Seed should be sown thinly in shallow drills early in the spring when the trees are starting out in leaf; and when the young plants are well started they should be thinned out or transplanted to stand six inches apart in the row. A second planting should be made about the first of August, which will furnish the largest and finest flowers of the season during the cool, fall months. **Faxon's Improved Sweet Mignonette will grow and thrive anywhere.**

Faxon's Improved SWEET MIGNONETTE SEED.

Price, Per Large Packet, 10 Cents ; 3 Packets for 25 Cents ; 10 Packets for 75 Cents ; 1-4 Ounce, 25 Cents ; Ounce, 75 Cents.

13

New Cockscomb—Ostrich Feather.

This new Feathered Celosia produces very large plumes, which are exquisitely curved and curled in exact resemblance of an ostrich feather. The plant grows about three feet high, is of handsome pyramidal form and the numerous massive plumes waving gracefully above the foliage **make it one of the most effective ornamental plants for either pot or outdoor culture.** It is of easy cultivation, requiring the same treatment as the ordinary cockscomb.

SUPERB MIXTURE. Beautiful shades of Crimson and Orange; the plumes are very large and exquisitely curved and curled.

PKT. 15 CTS.; 2 PKTS. FOR 25 CTS.

CROZY'S NEW DWARF CANNAS.

These new Dwarf Ever-blooming Large-flowering French Cannas **flower freely the first year from Seed.** Besides a large area growing for seed and roots, we have also had for ornament on the lawn, four beds of different named varieties, which have made a grand display for months, and now, at this writing (the middle of October), are still brilliant in bloom and bright in foliage. They are much less expensive (considering that they multiply rapidly both from roots and seed) and incomparably more beautiful for bedding than the best geraniums. In fact, we cannot recall any other plants that have ever given us such satisfaction in masses or beds, while even single specimens are most attractive in the garden. The roots can be kept in the cellar over winter and each clump will give six to eight good roots for planting out the following spring, when they will come quickly into flower. The **MIXED SEED** we offer has been saved from the finest varieties of all colors.

PER PKT. 10 CTS.; 3 PKTS. FOR 25 CTS.; OZ. 75 CTS.

GOLDEN GATE POPPIES.

Recall to mind every color you have ever seen in Poppies, then imagine every conceivable combination of colors—striped, blotched, edged, and bordered—on both single, semi-double, and double flowers, and you will have but a faint idea of the wondrously varied beauty of the new Golden Gate Poppies. No sight the past summer excited more attention nor called forth more expressions of wonder and amazement than our large block of these Poppies,—with thousands of open flowers of which seemingly there were no two alike.

They are also remarkable for their early and free-flowering habit—they are gorgeously brilliant throughout June and July.

PER PKT. 10 CTS.; 3 PKTS. FOR 25 CTS.

NEW COCKSCOMB—OSTRICH FEATHER.

The New Giant-Flowering Cosmos.

The flowers of this superb new strain are of immense size, measuring from 4½ to 5 inches across, and are produced in great diversity of form and coloring. In the mixture are monster pink and white flowers, beautiful crimson shades, delicate white and mauve; white, daintily tinted and clouded with pink and mauve. Some of the large white blossoms have broad plaited petals, with pinked edges, resembling the *Romneya Coulteri*, or California Tree Poppy, while immense pink and white flowers, with overlapping petals, resemble Camellias, although larger and more beautiful. The colors range from pure white through shades of pink, deep rose and crimson, to light red. Of the latter there are many dark shades heretofore unknown in Cosmos. There are white ones, delicately flushed or flecked with pink or mauve, and very beautiful flowers in pink and mauve have a dark red ring around the eye.

SUPERB MIXTURE. Embraces every shade from pure white to deep rose and crimson; commences blooming in July and continues in full flower until killed by the frost.
PKT. 15 CTS.; 2 PKTS. FOR 25 CTS.; ¼ OZ. $1.50; OZ. $5.00.

THE NEW GIANT-FLOWERING COSMOS.

14

NEW GRAND IMPERIAL
Japanese Morning Glories.

Gigantic Flowers, Exquisite New Colors, Magnificent Foliage.

The surpassing charm of these **Imperial Japanese Morning Glories** lies in the entrancing beauty and gigantic size of the flowers; they measure from four to six inches across, and their greater substance causes them to remain open much longer than ordinary Morning Glories. The colors of the flowers, shadings and markings are **limitless**, and are really wonders of nature, of such incomparable beauty that descriptions are inadequate. **Wherever climbers can be grown these should have a prominent place.** Some flowers are of deep, rich velvety tones, others more daintily tinted and shaded than an artist's brush could portray. The solid colors range through reds from soft rose to crimson, bronze and garnet maroon; from daintiest light blue to ultramarine indigo and blackish purple; from snow white to cream and silver gray; some are striped, starred and spotted; others have magnificent edges and throats. The double-flowering sorts are superb and must be seen to be appreciated to their full value.

SUPERB MIXTURE. My special mixture of all the very best double and single-flowering sorts—a grand assortment. **PKT. 15 CTS.; 2 PKTS. FOR 25 CTS.; OZ. $1.00.**

IMPERIAL JAPANESE MORNING GLORIES.

Datura, "Golden Queen."

This superb new variety has all the fine qualities of the popular *Datura cornucopia*, but on account of its brilliant yellow flowers it is a much more showy and effective plant. From seed sown in the open ground, it grows in a single season to a height of 2½ feet, forming a stocky, very bushy and compact plant, requiring no support. The flowers are of gigantic size, many of them 10 inches long, very double, and produced in great numbers. It makes a magnificent pot plant, and is admirably adapted for massing and backgrounds, the large bright flowers contrasting strikingly with the dark green foliage. **PER PKT., 10 CTS.; 3 PKTS. FOR 25 CTS.**

DATURA, "GOLDEN QUEEN."

CROTOLARIA RETUSA.
(WEST-INDIA RATTLE BOX.)

West=India Rattle Box. (Crotolaria Retusa.)

This is undoubtedly one of the most beautiful, interesting and easily grown plants in existence. It is a low-growing, profusely branching plant, every branch and branchlet ending in racemes 6 to 10 inches long, of beautiful, large, sweet-pea-like flowers. These flowers are of thick substance, fragrant, and in color golden yellow, except the keel in the centre, which looks like brown velvet, and are followed by clusters of short, smooth pods, in which, when shaken, the seeds sound like a child's rattle, hence its common name. In Florida it is known locally as Yellow Sweet Pea. **Although a perennial, it blooms the first year from seed, and in the garden may be treated as an annual.** In a temperate climate the seed should be sown in a frame or hot-house. **PKT. 10 CTS.; 3 PKTS. FOR 25 CTS.**

15

My Beautiful Wild=Flower Garden.

Full of Dainty Surprises————Over 100 Sorts For 20 Cents.

The introduction of these has proved a most marked success. Anyone who has planted and cultivated flowers in neatly laid-out beds is aware of the amount of labor and constant attention necessary to produce the desired effect. To those who cannot give this care, the "Wild Garden" presents a substitute which, for its unusual and varied effects, for cheapness and the small amount of labor necessary for its construction, has no rival. "Wild-Garden Seeds" are a mixture of over one hundred varieties of hardy flower seeds. **No one who has not seen such a garden can form an idea of its possibilities, the different seasons of bloom insuring something new almost every day.**

MIXED FLOWER SEEDS for
MY WILD=FLOWER or CHILDREN'S GARDEN.

This mixture embraces over one hundred varieties of the easiest growing flowers, producing a constant and varied bloom the whole season. For sowing in shrubbery, under trees and in beds on which no care will be bestowed, or even for sowing in exposed situations, where wildness is preferred to order and precision, "Wild-Garden Seeds" have no rival. This mixture comprises Mignonette, Candytuft, Larkspurs, Pansies, Balsams, Petunias, Phloxes, Marigolds, Poppies, Foxgloves and many other garden favorites, which will flower successively and yield an abundance of bloom. Many would like a few flowers, but cannot spare the time to give the necessary culture. These look out for themselves. It is also just the thing for the children's garden; besides yielding "the little people" a great deal of pleasure, it will prove most instructive — as almost every day there will be a new flower in bloom for them to find a name for. **The children always want their own individual flower gardens; and for this purpose there is nothing so good, or as cheaply purchased as "Wild-Garden Seeds."**

PRICES FOR
WILD-GARDEN SEEDS.

My Extra Choice Mixture contains over one hundred varieties of splendid, easily grown flowers; and will give the greatest satisfaction.

Half-ounce packet 20 cts.
6 (½ ounce) packets for $1.00.
One dozen (½ ounce) packets for $1.75.
Quarter-pound (in bulk) $1.00.
Pound (in bulk) $3.00.

☞ My packets of "Wild-Garden Seeds" are most attractive — the envelopes, containing the seeds, are beautifully illuminated, in many colors; having been specially imported from one of the best German lithographers.

☞ Much pleasure can be given in any village, by distributing a dozen packets of these "Wild-Garden Seeds"; to those "cottagers," who do not now have any flower garden. ☜

16

Standard Flower Seeds

I have this season most carefully revised my list of Flower Seeds, discarded all undesirable varieties, and added many recent introductions that I have found by thorough trials to be valuable acquisitions. **None but popular and reliable sorts are offered,** and I feel sure my customers will find this list very convenient to make up their orders from for the coming year.

On all orders for flower or vegetable seeds in packets or ounces, the purchaser may select seeds to the value of **$1.25** for each one dollar sent me. Thus, anyone sending $1.00 can select seeds in packets or ounces amounting to $1.25; for $2.00, seeds in packets or ounces to the value of $2.50, and so on. *This discount applies only to seeds IN PACKETS AND OUNCES.*

There are many varieties in the following list of such **UNQUESTIONED SUPERIORITY,** that no flower garden could be considered complete without them. That you may not overlook these flowers when making up your orders—YOU WILL FIND THESE SORTS INCLOSED IN RULES, AND THUS DESIGNATED.

ABRONIA. An elegant trailing plant, producing showy blossoms in dense verbena-like clusters. Flowers delicately perfumed. *Hardy Annuals.*
Umbellata. Rosy-lilac, pkt. 5 cts.
Arenaria. Yellow, fine, pkt. 10 cts.
ABUTILON (*Flowering Maple*). Very showy, decorative, and free-growing shrubs, both for the greenhouse and garden; easily grown from seed. *Half-hardy Shrubs.*
Extra Choice Mixed. Very choice sorts, 4 ft., pkt. 15 cts.
ACACIA. Very free-flowering shrubs, with handsome foliage and long spikes of globular flowers which are mostly yellow. Excellent window plants. *Half-hardy Shrubs.*
Mixed Varieties. Many sorts mixed, 3 to 10 ft., pkt. 10 cts.
ACHILLEA, The Pearl. A good border plant, producing abundant charming small double white flowers. *Hardy Perennial.* 1½ ft., pkt. 15 cts.
ACROCLINIUM. Elegant half-hardy annuals with "everlasting" flower heads, much used in bouquets of dried flowers. *Half-hardy Annuals.*
Single Varieties Mixed. Rose and white, 1 ft., pkt. 5 cts.
Double Varieties Mixed. Rose and white, 1 ft., pkt. 10 cts.
ADLUMIA (*Mountain Fringe*). A very desirable climbing plant with delicate foliage; flowers profusely all summer. *Hardy Biennials.*
Cirrhosa. Beautiful pink, 10 to 15 ft., pkt. 10 cts.
ADONIS. Handsome border plants of the easiest cultivation; the perennial species are very ornamental.
Æstivalis (*Hardy Annual*). Flowers crimson, 1 ft., pkt. 5 cts.
Vernalis (*Hardy Perennial*). Bright yellow, 1½ ft., pkt. 5 cts.
AGERATUM. Very useful plants for garden decoration or winter blooming in the house. Easily grown from seed and remain a long time in bloom. *Half-hardy Annual.*

AGERATUM—MEXICANUM. A very free-flowering variety, and most profuse bloomer; color beautiful lavender blue, 1½ ft.
Pkt. 5 cts.; oz. 40 cts.

Mexicanum Album. White, 1½ ft., pkt. 5 cts.
AGROSTEMMA. Very handsome border plants, free-flowering and easily grown in any garden; excellent for cut flowers as well. *Hardy Annuals.*
Mixed Varieties. Various colors, 1 ft., pkt. 5 cts.

ALONSOA, Grandiflora (*Mask Flower*). Free-flowering bedding plants, with handsome scarlet flowers, blooming profusely until frost. *Annual.* 2 ft., pkt. 5 cts.
ALYSSUM. Too well known to need any description, excellent for beds, borders or the rockery; the perennial sorts are much admired. All varieties are very easily grown and bloom abundantly. *Hardy Annuals except as noted.*

SWEET ALYSSUM. The well-known variety so much used in every garden, especially for edgings. White in color and very fragrant, ¾ ft. **Pkt. 5 cts.; oz. 40 cts.**

Saxatile Compactum (*Golden Alyssum*). Yellow, fine for edgings and borders. *Hardy Perennial.* ¾ ft., pkt. 5 cts.
Little Gem. Very compact and spreading, white, ¼ ft., pkt. 10 cts.
AMARANTHUS. Ornamental foliage plants with pretty flowers, of the easiest culture; are fine anywhere, either for bedding, vases, conservatory or pots. *Half-hardy Annuals.*
Caudatus (*Love-Lies-Bleeding*). Long red panicles, 3 ft., pkt. 5 cts.
Cruentus (*Prince's Feather*). Scarlet, very ornamental, 3½ ft., pkt. 5 cts.
Salicifolius (*Fountain Plant*). Highly decorative, 3 ft., pkt. 5 cts.
Tricolor (*Joseph's Coat*). Yellow, red and green foliage, 2 ft., pkt. 5 cts.

BEST MIXED AMARANTHUS
Very valuable bedding plants, as their beautifully variegated foliage is most ornamental. This is a very choice mixture, 2 to 4 ft.
Pkt. 5 cts.; oz. 25 cts.

AMPELOPSIS, Veitchii (*Japanese or Boston Ivy*). The fast growing and very ornamental climbing ivy, so much seen around Boston; clings firmly to stone or brick without fastening. *Hardy Perennial.* Grows quickly. Pkt. 10 cts.; oz. 50 cts.
ANAGALLIS (*Pimpernelle*). A very pretty and free-flowering trailing plant, useful for edgings, rustic baskets and rockwork. We offer a very fine mixture of colors. *Half-hardy Annual.* Pkt. 5 cts.
ANCHUSA, Capensis. Dwarf pretty plant, azure-blue, splendid for bouquets; Forget-me-not like flowers. *Hardy Annual.* 1 ft., pkt. 5 cts.

17

ANEMONE, Coronaria (*Wind-Flower*). Garden anemones are favorites with all, blooming early in the spring and being easily cultivated. Our mixture includes the choicest colors. *Hardy Perennial.* ½ ft., pkt. 10 cts.

ANTIRRHINUM (*Snap-Dragon*). A beautiful border plant, flowering abundantly the first summer from seed until after frost; also with a little protection blooms well the next season. Very showy, should be in every garden. *Half-hardy Perennial.*

FINEST MIXED SNAP-DRAGON. A splendid assortment of this popular border plant. Blooms continually from early summer until frost, 2 ft.
Pkt. 5 cts.

Dwarf Mixed (*Tom Thumb Varieties*). Charming for dwarf beds and edgings; these deserve a place in your garden. ¾ ft., pkt. 10 cts.

SUPERB AQUILEGIAS (*Columbine*). Too much praise can scarcely be lavished upon these elegant **hardy plants**, so easily grown from seed. They remain in bloom a long time and are very ornamental. My mixture embraces both double and single varieties in elegant assortment. *Hardy Perennials.* 1½ ft.
Pkt. 10 cts.; 3 pkts. for 25 cts.; oz. $1.00.

ASTERS. Asters are such universal favorites and so extensively grown for late summer and autumn flowering that it is unnecessary to say a single word in their praise. **As you know, we have for years made a specialty of asters, and we are convinced that our seed is the finest obtainable.** A rich, loamy soil is best, and as the roots are produced near the surface, a mulching of rotten manure is very beneficial. We earnestly advise all to plant generously of these magnificent annuals. *Half-hardy Annuals.*

Dwarf Chrysanthemum-Flowered. Large double flowers produced in clusters, very delicate and beautiful; mixed colors, ¾ ft., pkt. 10 cts.

Comet. Flowers with curled petals like Japanese chrysanthemums, large and double; all shades mixed, 1½ ft., pkt. 15 cts.

Mignon. Excellent class resembling the Victoria race, but still more floriferous, they keep a long time fresh; mixed colors, 1½ ft., pkt. 15 cts.

Large Rose-Flowered. A handsome large flowering class of great brilliancy; all colors mixed, 2 ft., pkt. 10 cts.; oz. $3.00.

VICTORIA ASTERS. Considered by many the most popular class in cultivation, adapted for any purpose, elegant large double flowers; our splendid mixture is unrivalled, 2 ft. **Large pkt. 25 cts.; 5 pkts. for $1.00; oz. $5.00.**

Washington. The largest flowered aster grown, especially prized for exhibition purposes; elegant mixture, 2 ft., pkt. 15 cts.

IMBRICATED POMPON ASTERS. Very free-flowering class with small flowers which are excellent for bouquets; our splendid mixture embraces every color, 2 ft. **Large pkt. 25 cts.; 5 pkts. for $1.00; oz. $5.00.**

Ball or Jewel. New class with short petals and perfectly round flowers; mixed colors, 2 ft., pkt. 15 cts.

Truffaut's Pæony-Flowered Perfection Asters. To our mind the best all-round aster in cultivation, flowers large and very brilliant; our splendid mixture includes all desirable shades, 2 ft. **Large pkt. 25 cts.; 5 pkts. for $1.00; oz. $5.00.**

Betteridge' Quilled. The best quilled aster, large flowers of all colors. 2 ft., pkt. 5 cts.

FAXON'S ROYAL MIXED ASTERS. Our splendid mixture of Perfection, Victoria, and Pompon varieties; this seed represents the highest perfection in asters, 2 ft. **Large pkt. 25 cts.; 5 pkts. for $1.00; oz. $5.00.**

Boston Florists' Double White Asters. Best pure white for cut flowers, 2 ft.
Pkt. 15 cts.; 8 pkts. for $1.00; oz. $4.00.

China Asters. A choice mixture of many varieties. 2 ft., pkt. 5 cts., oz. $1.50.
(*See "Faxon's Specialties" also.*)

BALSAMS (*Lady's Slipper*). A well-known and very ornamental annual, one of the showiest of our summer and autumn flowers, and well deserves a place in every garden; of easy cultivation but requires for best results very rich soil. *Half-hardy Annual.* 2 ft.

DOUBLE CAMELLIA-FLOWERED BALSAMS My best mixture of these magnificent summer-flowering favorites; producing masses of large, double blooms of most brilliant colors and in the greatest profusion. **Pkt. 15 cts.; 2 pkts. for 25 cts.; ¼ oz. 50 cts.; oz. $1.50.**

Double Rose-Flowered. Very double, the best balsam for florists; our strain includes all the best colors. Pkt. 10 cts., oz. $1.50.

Boston Florists'. The best pure white for florists. Pkt. 10 cts., oz. $1.50.

Fine Mixed. Many good sorts mixed, pkt. 5 cts., oz. 60 cts.

BALLOON VINE (*Love-in-a-Puff*). A rapid-growing climber with pretty foliage and white flowers. *Hardy Annual.* 10 ft., pkt. 5 cts.

BARTONIA, Aurea. Any ordinary garden soil suits this flower, splendid for beds or borders, very showy and well worth growing; a beautiful golden yellow. *Hardy Annual.* 1 ft., pkt. 5 cts.

BEGONIA. One of our most beautiful summer and autumn flowering plants, of easy culture and of most gorgeous colors; half shade is the best situation for the plants. *Greenhouse Perennial.* ¾ ft.

Double Mixed (*tuberous-rooted*). An unrivalled strain; choice mixed colors, pkt. 50 cts.

Single Mixed (*tuberous-rooted*). All the best colors mixed, pkt. 35 cts.

Rex Varieties. The beautiful ornamental-leaved sorts; mixed, pkt. 25 cts.

BELLIS PERENNIS (*Double Daisy*). The handsome double daisy, a fine flower for spring blooming; seed sown early, flowers first season. *Hardy Perennial.*

Double White. Purest white, pkt. 15 cts.; oz. $5.00.

Longfellow. Dark rose, large and double, pkt. 15 cts.

Extra Choice Mixed. Finest mixed double sorts, pkt. 15 cts.; oz. $5.00.

BRACHYCOME (*Swan-River-Daisy*). Pretty little plants with single daisy-like flowers. *Hardy Annual.* ¾ ft.
Mixed Varieties. Many sorts, pkt. 5 cts.

BROWALLIA, Extra Fine Mixed. Handsome garden plants with blue and white flowers, also excellent for pot culture in winter. *Half-hardy Annual.* 1½ ft., pkt. 5 cts.

CACALIA (*Tassel Flower*). Free-flowering plants of the easiest culture, with tassel-like blooms. *Hardy Annual.* 1½ ft.
Aurea. Golden yellow, pkt. 5 cts.; oz. 50 cts.
Coccinea. Orange scarlet, pkt. 5 cts.; oz. 50 cts.

CALCEOLARIA, Finest Mixed Varieties. Finest varieties in cultivation of this most beautiful house plant, very large blooms of every conceivable color. *Tender Perennial.* 1 to 1½ ft., pkt. 50 cts.

CALENDULA (*Pot Marigold*). Very showy and profuse flowering, good in any situation indoors or out; the newer sorts are truly grand, and bloom throughout the season. *Hardy Annual.* 1½ ft.
Le Proust. Nankeen-colored, very double, pkt. 5 cts.; oz. 20 cts.

Meteor. Striped double flowers of light orange, pkt. 5 cts.; oz. 20 cts.

CALENDULA.

PRINCE OF ORANGE. A very showy sort and most profuse bloomer. In color it is a splendid dark orange; very double and large.
Pkt. 5 cts.; oz. 25 cts.

(See Marigolds also.)

CALLIOPSIS or COREOPSIS. Largely grown for beds and borders, also splendid cut flowers; colors very rich and beautiful, in fact one of our best garden plants. *Hardy Annual.*
Bicolor. Yellow and brown, pkt. 5 cts.; oz. 30 cts.
Coronata. Yellow, with crimson spots, pkt. 5 cts.; oz. 30 cts.
Drummondii (*Golden Wave*). Golden yellow, dark center, pkt. 5 cts.; oz. 30 cts.
Finest Mixed. All the best sorts, pkt. 5 cts.; oz. 30 cts.

CAMPANULA MEDIUM (*Canterbury Bells.*) Few indeed of our hardy plants are more desirable than these, easily grown and very showy; with brilliant bell-shaped blooms of many colors. *Hardy Biennal.* 2½ ft.
Double Mixed. Very choicest shades, pkt. 10 cts.
Single Mixed. All the best sorts, pkt. 5 cts.

CANARY-BIRD FLOWER (*Tropæolum Canariense*). A beautiful climber with bright yellow flowers. *Hardy Annual.* 10 ft., pkt. 10 cts.; oz. 60 cts.

CANDYTUFT. One of our best garden plants doing well in ordinary soil, flowers freely and blooms until frost. *Hardy Annual* except as noted. 1 ft.
Dark Crimson. The darkest variety, pkt. 5 cts.; oz. 25 cts.
White Rocket. Large white heads, pkt. 5 cts.; oz. 20 cts.
Fragrant White. White and sweet scented, pkt. 5 cts.; oz. 25 cts.
Purple. Fine for bedding, pkt. 5 cts.; oz. 25 cts.

CANDYTUFT—BEST MIXTURE.

An elegant mixture of this most useful and perfectly hardy annual. Very free-flowering and includes the richest and most brilliant colors.
Pkt. 5 cts.; oz. 25 cts.

Sempervirens (*Perennial*). Best hardy variety; white, pkt. 10 cts.

CANNAS (*Indian Shot*). The well-known ornamental foliage plant, easily grown from seed, which should be soaked before sowing; do nicely in pots in winter also. *Half-hardy Perennial.*

CROZY'S NEW DWARF CANNAS.

A choice mixture of these now most popular dwarf flowering varieties, 3 to 4 ft. Pkt. 10 cts.; oz. 75 cts.

Finest Mixed. Light and dark leaved sorts, 6 ft., pkt. 5 cts; oz. 40 cts.

CARNATIONS. Our strains of these popular greenhouse and window plants are unsurpassed; also very desirable plants for garden culture in summer; deliciously fragrant and of most brilliant colors. *Half-hardy Perennials.* 1 to 1½ ft.
Choicest Double Mixed. Our best assortment. pkt. 50 cts.
Very Fine Mixed. Very choice sorts, pkt. 25 cts.
Perpetual or Tree. Best double varieties of this fine winter flowering carnation; an elegant mixture, pkt. 50 cts.

NEW "MARGUERITE" CARNATIONS.

This new class has justified the highest expectations. With the simplest culture they *will bloom in four months after sowing the seed;* and do equally well in the open garden or in pots; our strain represents the very best colors and is of such vigorous, dwarf, erect growth that no supports are required. The individual flowers have long, strong stems, and are exquisitely sweet. ALL COLORS MIXED.
Per pkt. 10 cts.; 3 pkts. for 25 cts.; 10 pkts. for 75 cts.; ¼ oz. 75 cts.; oz. $2.50.

(See also Dianthus and Sweet William.)

CELOSIA (*Cockscomb*). Strikingly brilliant for the summer garden or as winter pot plants, require good sandy loam for best results; the flower heads often measure ten inches across. *Hardy Annuals.*
Dwarf Mixed. Includes many fine shades of red, ¾ ft., pkt. 5 cts.

COCKSCOMB—GLASGOW PRIZE.

For mixing with other plants to give color and striking effect to our flower beds; I know no plant its equal—it is simply grand. Is very dwarf and produces most beautiful crimson combs; foliage dark green.
Pkt. 10 cts.; 3 pkts. for 25 cts.; oz. $2.50.

Tall Mixed. The very best of the tall varieties, 2 ft., pkt. 5 cts.

CENTAUREA. Easily cultivated, showy plants; the silvery leaved sorts are much used for borders; the beautiful bachelor's button needs no description.

BACHELOR'S BUTTON.

CENTAUREA CYANUS (*Blue Bottle or Corn Flower*). Needs no description; is planted by every one. My mixture of this old-fashioned flower is very fine, and universally admired. *Annual.* 2 ft. Pkt. 5 cts.; oz. 25 cts.

Double Cyanus. New double sorts, mixed colors. *Annual.* 2 ft., pkt. 10 cts.
Moschata (*Sweet Sultan*). Mixed colors of this free-flowering favorite. *Annual.* 1½ ft., pkt. 5 cts.
Candidissima (*Dusty Miller*). Thick silvery foliage. *Perennial.* ¾ ft., pkt. 15 cts.; 1,000 seeds, $1.00.
Gymnocarpa (*Dusty Miller*). Very graceful silvery foliage. *Perennial.* 1 ft., pkt. 10 cts.; oz. 80 cts.

CENTRANTHUS, Finest Mixed. Pretty, compact growing. *Hardy Annual.* 1½ ft., pkt. 5 cts.

CHRYSANTHEMUMS. This family of plants embraces many varieties, all of which are much prized; the annual sorts are easily grown and very pretty in any garden; the "Paris Daisies" and "Perennial" varieties all are familiar with, as pot-plants and cut flowers.

ANNUAL CHRYSANTHEMUMS.

SUPERB MIXTURE. This is a splendid mixture of all the best double and single annual varieties. This class is very desirable for the summer garden; being very showy, free bloomers, and should be grown in large beds, where they will show their bright colors finely, 1½ ft.
Pkt. 10 cts.; 3 pkts. for 25 cts.; oz. $1.00.

Frutescens (*White Marguerite*). This beautiful *greenhouse* variety makes a most elegant pot-plant, as well as flowering all summer in the open ground; this is the *White Paris Daisy.* 1½ ft., pkt. 10 cts.

PERENNIAL CHRYSANTHEMUMS.

These are the popular varieties so much grown for Fall and Winter blooming in pots; also for cut-flowers. I offer an elegant mixture of all the very finest varieties, including the best *Chinese, Japanese,* and *Pompon* sorts. This seed will give you grand results.
Per pkt. 25 cts.; 5 pkts. for $1.00.

CINERARIA. The cineraria is one of our most prized house plants, blooming as they do so profusely and continuously during the late winter and spring months. *Tender Perennial.* 1½ ft.
Extra Choice Mixed. Best sorts in cultivation, extra fine, pkt. 50 cts.
Double Flowering. Best mixed colors, pkt. 50 cts.

CLARKIA. Elegant slender branching plants, largely grown on account of their extreme showiness and easy culture. *Hardy Annual.* 1 ft.
Finest Mixed. Best double and single sorts, mixed, pkt. 5 cts.; oz. 50 cts.

CLEMATIS (*Virgin's Bower*). One of our best climbing shrubs, admirably adapted for covering stumps, arbors or rock-work; we offer a very choice mixture of the best varieties. *Hardy Perennial.* 10 to 25 ft., pkt. 10 cts.; oz. 50 cts.

CLIANTHUS (*Glory Pea*). A splendid free-blooming climbing shrub with brilliant scarlet flowers. *Tender Perennial.* 4 ft.

Dampieri. The best variety, pkt. 25 cts.

COBÆA, Scandens. A popular, rapid growing climber with purple flowers and beautiful foliage. *Half-hardy Perennial.* 25 ft., pkt. 10 cts. ; oz. 80 cts.

COLEUS. This ornamental leaved bedding plant is found in every garden, also very desirable for pot-culture in winter; very easily grown from seed. *Half-hardy Perennial.* 1½ ft.

Extra Choice Mixed. Saved from best varieties, pkt. 25 cts.

CONVOLVULUS (*Morning Glory*). The tall varieties are splendid climbers, with beautiful bright flowers; the dwarf sorts have equally handsome blooms and are excellent for beds or borders. *Hardy Annuals.*

Tall Mixed. Containing all the best colors, 15 ft., pkt. 5 cts. ; oz. 15 cts.

Dwarf Mixed. Splendid mixture for beds and borders. 1 ft., pkt. 5 cts. ; oz. 25 cts.

(*See Cypress Vine and Ipomœa also.*)

COSMOS. Very valuable plant for late summer flowering, grows five feet high, resembling a single dahlia; very profuse bloomer and easily grown. *Hardy Annual.* 5 ft.

White Pearl. Excellent for cut flowers. Pkt. 10 cts. ; oz. 80 cts.

Choice Mixed. All colors mixed, pkt. 10 cts. ; oz. 80 cts.

CUPHEA, Platycentra (*Cigar* or *Fire-Cracker Plant*). Scarlet, very pretty plant, excellent *Perennial* for pot-culture. 1 ft., pkt. 10 cts.

CYCLAMEN. Most charming bulbous-rooted plants with beautiful foliage, flowers of very brilliant colors; one of our very best pot-plants for winter blooming. *Greenhouse Bulbs.* ¾ ft.

Persicum, Extra Choice Mixed. Very best varieties, pkt. 35 cts.

CYPRESS VINE. One of the most elegant climbing vines; delicate, fernlike foliage, and beautiful, star-shaped flowers. *Half-hardy Annual.* 15 ft.

Scarlet. Very brilliant scarlet, pkt. 5 cts. ; oz. 40 cts.

White. Purest white, a great favorite, pkt. 5 cts. ; oz. 40 cts.

Finest Mixed. All colors in mixture, pkt. 5 cts. ; oz. 30 cts.

(*See Convolvulus and Ipomœa also.*)

DAHLIAS. If sown early these stately fall flowers can be raised very easily from seed. Our mixtures are unsurpassed, containing the very choicest colors. *Half-hardy Perennial.* 3 to 5 ft.

Choicest Double Mixed. A superb mixture of the best double varieties, pkt. 15 cts.

NEW SINGLE DAHLIAS.

A very beautiful and extremely dwarf single strain, growing only from 10 to 15 inches high, and flowering the first season from seed. In fact it begins to bloom in June and flowers profusely until frost comes in October. A most valuable bedding plant for our gardens; and also splendid for cultivation in pots. My Mixture contains many elegant colors and is very fine.

Pkt. 15 cts.; 2 pkts. for 25 cts.; oz. $2.00.

DATURA (*Trumpet Flower*), **Mixed.** A pretty and easily grown bushy plant bearing large, fragrant trumpet-shaped flowers. *Hardy Annual.* 3 ft., pkt. 5 cts.

DELPHINIUM (*Perennial Larkspur*). Choice Mixed. Best mixture of both double and single hardy sorts, 2 ft., pkt. 15 cts.

(*For Annual Varieties see Larkspur.*)

DIANTHUS (*Pinks.*) The China and Japan Pinks have always been favorites, and deservedly so, as their brilliant blooms and dwarf bushy habit render them unsurpassed for beds and borders; also one of the best plants for cut flowers. No garden is complete without a generous supply. *Hardy Annuals* except as noted. 1 ft.

DOUBLE CHINESE PINKS

(*Chinensis fl. pl.*). Also known as Indian Pink; a splendid mixture of the very choicest colors of this most popular flower. Should be planted liberally in every garden. **Pkt. 5 cts.; oz. 40 cts.**

Double Diadem Pink (*Diadematus fl. pl.*). Very large double flowers, all colors mixed, pkt. 10 cts.; oz. $1.50.

Heddewigi (*Japan Pink*). Finest selected single-flowered, mixed. Unquestionably one of our finest annuals. Pkt. 5 cts. ; oz. $1.00.

Double Heddewigi. A splendid mixture of the double sorts of the *Japan Pink*, pkt. 5 cts. ; oz. $1.00.

DIANTHUS—SUPERB MIXTURE.

Every season it seems as if *Garden Pinks* were becoming more popular; and deservedly so, as few flowers can equal them in beauty and profusion of bloom. This is a grand collection; comprising all varieties of the Chinese and Japanese Pinks, including both large-flowering single and double sorts. Most easily raised from seed; and will flower continually from early summer until late autumn. This is an elegant mixture of "everything in pinks" and will be one of the features of your garden.

Pkt. 10 cts.; 3 pkts. for 25 cts.; ¼ oz. 40 cts.; oz. $1.50.

Laciniatus. A beautiful double fringed variety, mixed colors, pkt. 10 cts. ; oz. $1.25.

Imperialis (*Double Imperial Pink*). Extra fine mixture of these charming varieties, pkt. 5 cts. ; oz. $1.00.

HARDY CLOVE PINKS

(*Hardy Garden Pinks*). A splendid free-flowering class, having a strong clove fragrance; my mixture is composed of many splendid colors of both double and semi-double varieties. These pinks are also well known as *Pheasant-Eye* or *Grass Pinks*, and being hardy are very desirable. Fine for cut-flowers.

Pkt. 15 cts.; 2 pkts. for 25 cts.; oz. $5.00.

(*See also Carnations and Sweet William.*)

DIGITALIS (*Foxglove*), **Fine Mixed.** Long racemes of beautiful spotted flowers, very ornamental. *Hardy Perennial.* 3 ft., pkt. 5 cts.

DOLICHOS (*Hyacinth Bean*), **Lablab.** A beautiful quick-growing climber with purple and white flowers in clusters. *Hardy Annual.* 15 ft., pkt. 5 cts. ; oz. 25 cts.

DRACÆNA, Finest Mixed. Ornamental foliage plants, extensively used for the centers of vases and for pot-culture. *Tender Perennial.* 3 ft. All the best sorts, pkt. 25 cts.

ECHEVERIA, Fine Mixed. Succulent, free-growing plants, suitable for rockeries and edgings. *Tender Perennial.* ¼ to ½ ft., pkt. 25 cts.

ELICHRYSUM (*Everlasting Flowers*). Pretty garden plants, blooms extensively, used for winter bouquets; flowers that are intended for drying should be gathered when partially unfolded. *Hardy Annual.* 1½ to 2 ft.

Double and Single. All colors and varieties mixed, pkt. 10 cts.

ESCHSCHOLTZIA (*California Poppy*). These showy plants are largely employed in decorating beds and borders; in bloom all summer and fall; easily grown, flowers very handsome. *Hardy Annual.* 1 ft.

California. Bright yellow with orange center, pkt. 5 cts. ; oz. 40 cts.

Carminea (*Rose Cardinal*). Beautiful carmine, pkt. 5 cts. ; oz. 50 cts.

Mandarin. Deep orange, splendid, pkt. 5 cts. ; oz. 60 cts.

ESCHSCHOLTZIA.

SPLENDID MIXTURE. A very choice mixture of these splendid garden favorites; the flowers are large and of many bright colors. Besides being grand in the garden, these showy plants are very fine when grown in pots.

Pkt. 5 cts.; oz. 30 cts.

EUPHORBIA, Variegata (*Snow on the Mountain*). Ornamental foliage plant, leaves veined and margined with white. *Hardy Annual.* 2 ft., pkt. 5 cts.

FERNS, Mixed. A very nice mixture of all the best varieties for greenhouse or house culture. ½ to 2 ft., pkt. 25 cts.

Hardy Varieties. For out-door growing; a very choice assortment. 1 to 2 ft., pkt. 25 cts.

FORGET-ME-NOT (*Myosotis*). These charming little plants succeed well almost anywhere; one of our prettiest spring flowers. *Half-hardy Perennial,* blooming the first year from seed. ½ ft.
Palustris. The true marsh Forget-me-not, a beautiful blue. Pkt. 10 cts.
Victoria. New, of dwarf globular habit, sky blue flowers, the center ones double, the finest Forget-me-not for pot-culture. Pkt. 15 cts.; ¼ oz. $1.00. 10 cts.
Fine Mixed. A fine mixture of many sorts, pkt. 10 cts.

FUCHSIAS, Mixed. We offer a very choice assortment of double and single sorts in splendid mixture. Fuchsias are easily raised from seed flowering the first year. *Tender Perennial.* 1 to 2 ft., pkt. 25 cts.

GAILLARDIAS. Showy bedding plants, giving a profusion of large and brilliant flowers all through the summer and fall; the plants thrive in any situation. *Hardy Annuals,* 1½ ft.
Finest, Single Mixed. Very rich colors; a splendid mixture, pkt. 5 cts.; oz. 30 cts.
Double, Lorenziana (*New Double Gaillardia*). Excellent for bedding and cut flowers, a very rich mixture; always in bloom, an elegant annual. Pkt. 5 cts.; oz. 50 cents.

GERANIUMS (*Pelargonium*). These favorites are easily raised from seed, in fact new varieties are produced in this manner; our mixtures are very choice. *Greenhouse Perennial.* 1 to 1½ ft.
Finest Show Varieties. Saved from prize flowers, pkt. 50 cts.
Apple-Scented. Very fragrant leaves, pkt. 15 cts.

GILIA, Mixed. Very attractive dwarf plants for beds or edgings; showy flowers borne in clusters. *Hardy Annual.* 1 ft., pkt. 5 cts.

GLOBE AMARANTHUS (*Gomphrena*). **Mixed.** Showy, everlasting flowers; small double blooms of perfect form and brilliant colors. *Half-hardy Annuals.* 1½ ft., pkt. 5 cts.; oz. 30 cts.

GLOXINIAS. Easily grown from seed and one of our most beautiful house plants, flowers of varied and very brilliant colors; thrive best in sandy loam. *Tender Perennial.* 1 ft.
Extra Choice Mixed. Best sorts in cultivation, pkt. 50 cts.

GODETIAS, Finest Mixed. Very beautiful garden plants, splendid for borders or in masses, also make nice house plants; succeeding well in any situation. *Hardy Annual.* 1 ft. Very best mixture, pkt. 5 cts.; oz. 30 cts.

GOURDS (*Ornamental*). Rapid-growing climbing vines with ornamental foliage and producing a great variety of curious fruits of various colors. *Tender Annual.* 15 to 20 ft.
Fine Mixed Varieties. Including all the most desirable sorts, pkt. 10 cts.; oz. 50 cts.

GYPSOPHILA (*Baby's Breath*). A pretty little plant for borders or rockeries; thrives well anywhere even in a dryish soil.
Elegans (*Hardy Annual*). White, 1½ ft., pkt. 5 cts.
Paniculata (*Hardy Perennial*). A very elegant, light and graceful plant; beautiful foliage and most tiny white flowers. Splendid for bouquets especially for mixing with sweet peas. 1½ ft., pkt. 10 cts.

HELIANTHUS (*Sunflower*). Well-known showy plants of easy culture in almost any moderately good garden soil. *Hardy Annuals.*
Russian Mammoth. The very large sort, grown everywhere. 6 ft., pkt. 5 cts.; oz. 10 cts.

SUNFLOWER.

DOUBLE GLOBOSUS. An elegant, large, double variety of a most intense deep yellow color. Flowers globe-shaped; and the plants attain a height of about six feet. Very showy for backgrounds and shrubberies or as single specimens, 6 ft. **Pkt. 5 cts.; oz. 30 cts.**

Cucumerifolius. This is the *Miniature Sunflower;* makes a bushy plant covered with hundreds of brightest orange-yellow flowers. 4 ft., pkt. 5 cts.; oz. 40 cts.

HELIOTROPE.

SUPERB MIXTURE. Everybody likes heliotrope, but all may not know that it can be raised very easily from seed; flowering in August. My mixture contains all the desirable shades from white to the deepest blue—almost black; is deliciously fragrant and blooms most profusely. *Half-hardy Perennial.* 1 to 1½ ft.
Pkt. 10 cts.; 3 pkts. for 25 cts.

HIBISCUS, Africanus. Very showy and ornamental; large creamy-yellow flowers with brown center. *Hardy Annual.* 2 ft., pkt. 5 cts.

HOLLYHOCKS. For majestic growth and massive beauty this oldest garden favorite stands unrivalled. *My strain is of unsurpassed quality.* *Hardy Biennial.* 6 ft.

Faxon's "Massachusetts Prize" Hollyhocks

(*Exhibition Strain*). My best mixture; this seed has been saved from the very choicest double blooms of every conceivable shade and color.
Pkt. 15 cts.; 2 pkts. for 25 cts.; 10 pkts. for $1.00. Ounce $3.00. Plants $2.00 per dozen; $12.00 per hundred.

Choice Mixed. A fine mixture of double sorts, pkt. 10 cts.; oz. $1.25.
Single Mixed. Choice mixed single varieties that many so much admire, pkt. 15 cts.
(*See "Faxon's Specialties" also.*)

HONESTY (*Lunaria*), **Finest Mixed.** Very showy. *Hardy Biennial.* 2 ft., pkt. 5 cts.

HUMULUS, Japonicus (*Japanese Hop*). A rapid growing climber, beautiful for trellises or rustic work. *Hardy Annual.* 20 ft., pkt. 10 cts.

ICE PLANT. Fine trailing plant for baskets and vases; singular icy foliage. *Tender Annual.* Pkt. 5 cts.

IPOMŒA (*Convolvulus*). Rapid growing climbers very useful and beautiful either in the house or garden. *Hardy Annuals.* 10 to 25 ft.
Finest Double Mixed. A very choice assortment, pkt. 10 cts.
Coccinea (*Star Ipomœa*). Scarlet, very free bloomer, pkt. 5 cts.
Noctiflora (*Moon-Flower*). The large white variety so much grown of late, pkt. 10 cts.
(*See Convolvulus and Cypress Vine also.*)

LANTANA. Very desirable plants for pot-culture or the garden; of easy culture and remain in bloom a large part of the year, very easily raised from seed. *Greenhouse Shrub.* 1½ ft.
Finest Mixed Hybrids. A mixture of the best colors, pkt. 10 cts.

LARKSPUR (*Delphinium*). Well-known garden plants of great beauty and noted for brilliant colors and profusion of bloom. *Hardy Annuals.*
Double Dwarf Rocket. Best double sorts in mixture, 1 ft., pkt. 5 cts.; oz. 30 cts.

DOUBLE BRANCHING LARKSPUR.

A very choice mixture of this ornamental and showy flower. My strain is of erect, branching habit; and of rich and varied colors, 2 ft.
Pkt. 5 cts.; oz. 30 cts.

(*See Delphinium also.*)

LATHYRUS, Latifolius (*Perennial Peas*). We offer a very choice mixture of these beautiful hardy climbers. *Hardy Perennial.* 6 ft., pkt. 10 cts.

LAVENDULA (*Lavender*). Fragrant blue flowers. *Hardy Perennial.* 1 to 2 ft., pkt. 5 cts.

LINARIA, Mixed. An attractive and free-flowering annual. *Hardy Annual.* 1½ ft., pkt. 5 cts.

LINUM (*Flowering Flax*). Brilliant, dark crimson. *Hardy Annual.* 1¼ ft., pkt. 5 cts.

LOBELIA. Splendid for hanging baskets and vases; the dwarf sorts are indispensable for bedding arrangements, as no other plants can take their place for pretty blue edgings. *Annuals* except as noted.
Crystal Palace Compacta. Dark blue, the best sort for edgings, ½ ft.; pkt. 10 cts.

Gracilis. Light blue; slender trailing stems, the best variety for hanging baskets, pkt. 10 cts.
Fine Mixed. A choice mixture for bedding and borders, ½ ft., pkt. 10 cts.
Cardinalis (*Cardinal Flower*). Brilliant scarlet. *Hardy Perennial.* 2 ft., pkt. 10 cts.

LUPINS, Mixed. *Annual Varieties.* 3 ft., pkt. 5 cts.

LYCHNIS, Mixed. *Hardy Perennial.* 2 ft., pkt. 10 cts.

MARIGOLDS (*Tagetes*). Universally planted by everyone; the African varieties are stronger in habit and produce larger flowers than the French. The French sorts are beautifully mottled and velvety-flowered. *Hardy Annual.*

EL DORADO MARIGOLDS. This is the best strain of African Marigolds; the flowers are of enormous size, perfectly double and imbricated. The blooms run through all shades of yellow, from light lemon to the darkest orange, 2 ft. **Pkt. 5 cts.; oz. 60 cts.**

African, Finest Mixed. All colors in mixture, 2 ft., pkt. 5 cts.; oz. 40 cts.
French, Tall. Best mixed double varieties, 2 ft., pkt. 5 cts.; oz. 40 cts.

BEST FRENCH MARIGOLDS This strain is a very elegant mixture, of the best and most compact growing varieties, of the double flowering, dwarf French Marigolds. The flowers are perfectly double and of the finest colors—including the velvety shades. Very showy and effective, 1 ft. **Pkt. 5 cts.; oz. 50 cts.**

(*See Calendula also.*)

MARVEL-OF-PERU (*Mirabilis*). We have a very choice collection of these brilliant and showy flowers; the *Marvel-Of-Peru* or *Four-o'clock* will grow anywhere and is fine for beds or masses. *Hardy Annual.* 2 ft.
Choicest Mixed. A splendid assortment, pkt. 5 cts.; oz. 15 cts.

MATRICARIA (*Feverfew*). Pretty free-flowering dwarf plants with pure double white flowers; fine for bedding or pot-culture. *Hardy Annual.* ¾ ft.
Double Pure White. Purest white, pkt. 10 cts.

MAURANDYA, Finest Mixed. Beautiful climbers with elegant flowers and foliage, excellent for vases, window boxes and light trellises. *Half-hardy Perennial* but flowers the first season. 10 ft., pkt. 10 cts.

MESEMBRYANTHEMUM, Fine Mixed. *Annual.* ½ ft., pkt. 10 cts.

MIGNONETTE (*Reseda*). Sweet mignonette needs no introduction, it is a universal favorite; of the easiest culture, doing equally well in the garden or window box. *Hardy Annual.* 1 ft.

SWEET MIGNONETTE. The improved Sweet Mignonette is splendid. My strain is deliciously fragrant and produces very large flower spikes. **Pkt. 5 cts.; oz. 15 cts.**

Miles' Spiral. Long spikes, very fragrant, pkt. 5 cts.; oz. 40 cts.
Machet. Best for pot-culture, reddish, fragrant flowers, pkt. 10 cts.; oz. 75 cts.
Parson's White. Large white spikes, sweet scented, pkt. 5 cts.; oz. 40 cts.
Victoria. Large dark red flowers, very fragrant. pkt. 10 cts.; oz. 60 cts.

MIMULUS, Mixed (*Monkey-Flower*). *Hardy Perennial* varieties. 1 ft., pkt. 15 cts.

NASTURTIUMS. *I have for years made a specialty of these flowers and my strains of seed of the various types cannot be surpassed;* for full descriptions and cultural directions see my "specialty pages" in the first part of this catalogue. *Hardy Annuals.*

FAXON'S CHAMPION TALL MIXED. Finest tall or climbing varieties, 6 to 10 ft. **Pkt. 5 cts.; oz. 15 cts.; ¼ lb. 50 cts.; lb. $1.50.**

FAXON'S CHAMPION DWARF MIXED. Best Tom Thumb or dwarf sorts in cultivation, 1 to 1¼ ft. **Pkt. 5 cts.; oz. 25 cts.; ¼ lb. 75 cts.; lb. $2.50.**

FAXON'S LOBBIANUM VARIETIES. Splendid running sort, fine for arbors and rock-work; flowers strikingly brilliant, and in greatest variety of gorgeous colors. Runs 4 to 8 ft. **Pkt. 10 cts.; oz. 40 cts.; ¼ lb. $1.25; lb. $4.50.**

(*See "Faxon's Specialties" also.*)

NEMOPHILA. Pretty dwarf plants of the easiest culture, and admirably adapted for rockeries, borders and beds. *Hardy Annual.* 1 ft.
Fine Mixed. Including many choice colors, pkt. 5 cts.; oz. 30 cts.

NICOTIANA, Affinis. A favorite for pot-culture for the garden, flowers freely; white and fragrant. *Hardy Annual.* 2 ft., pkt. 10 cts.

NIGELLA (*Love-in-a-Mist or Devil-in-the-Bush*), **Finest Mixed.** *Hardy Annual.* 1 ft., pkt. 5 cts.

NOLANA, Mixed. Pretty trailing plant. *Hardy Annual.* 1 ft., pkt. 5 cts.

ŒNOTHERA (*Evening Primrose*), **Finest Mixed.** A showy *Hardy Annual.* 1 to 2 ft., pkt. 5 cts.

OXALIS, Choice Mixed. Pretty for hanging baskets. *Half-hardy Perennial.* ¾ ft., pkt. 10 cts.

PANSIES. Pansies have always been a specialty of mine, and it gives me much satisfaction to know from the reports of my customers that my seed is acknowledged to be the best obtainable. *Hardy Annuals.* **½ to ¾ ft.**

FAXON'S "WHITE HOUSE" PANSIES. My best mixture, for full description see specialty pages in the first part of this catalogue. **Pkt. 50 cts.; 5 pkts. for $2.00. Trade pkt. $1.00; 6 trade pkts. for $5.00; Ounce $15.00.**

Cassier's Blotched. Very large and beautifully blotched flowers; a very showy and especially rich strain, pkt. 40 cts.; 3 pkts. for $1.00.
Bugnot's Superb Varieties. Very beautiful large blooms with very broad blotches, the two upper petals finely lined; this mixture contains a great variety of very handsome colors. Pkt. 40 cts.; 3 pkts. for $1.00.
Giant Trimardeau. Beautiful class, the plants are of vigorous, compact growth; the flowers of good form and enormous size, a desirable mixture. Pkt. 15 cts.; ¼ oz. $1.25; oz. $4.50.

SUPERB PRIZE PANSIES. Having had many inquiries for a choice mixture of pansy seed,—I have composed this strain. It is a very rich and choicely varied mixture, and will be sure to give the greatest satisfaction. It produces the most elegant flowers of large size, and in the greatest variety. It is a splendid assortment at a very low price; and I know it will be sure to please. **Pkt. 15 cts.; 2 pkts. for 25 cts.; 10 pkts. for $1.00; ¼ oz. $2.50; oz. $9.00.**

Extra Choice Mixed. A very nice mixture, pkt. 10 cts.; 3 pkts. for 25 cts.; ¼ oz. 85 cts.; oz. $3.00.
Good Mixed. A good variety of colors, will make a nice bed in any garden, pkt. 5 cts.; ¼ oz. 40 cts.; oz. $1.50.

Large-Flowering Pansies in Separate Colors.

Black. Pkt. 15 cts.
Dark Blue. Pkt. 15 cts.
Red. Pkt. 15 cts.
Bronze. Pkt. 15 cts.
White. Pkt. 15 cts.
Fawn Color. Pkt. 15 cts.
Golden Yellow. Pkt. 15 cts.
Brown-Red. Pkt. 15 cts.
(*See "Faxon's Specialties" also.*)

PENTSTEMON, Fine Mixed. *Hardy Perennial.* 2 ft., pkt. 10 cts.

PERILLA, Nankinensis. A splendid dark-leaved foliage plant. *Hardy Annual.* 2 ft., pkt. 10 cts.

PETUNIAS. Petunias fill a place all their own in the garden border and are deservedly a favorite with us all. We have added many new varieties to our collection that we know will please our customers. *Hardy Annual.* 1 to 1½ ft.

Striped and Blotched. A large-flowering strain of most splendid colors. An unsurpassed mixture. Pkt. 10 cts.; ¼ oz. 75 cts.; oz. $2.50.

Superb Single Mixed. My best mixture of single-flowering petunias, a strain of incomparable beauty, size and luxuriance. Flowers most varied in color and markings, and of enormous size. Pkt. 25 cts.

Superb Double Mixed. My best mixture of all the large-flowering double varieties; including show, striped, blotched and fringed sorts; a most elegant assortment, pkt. 50 cts.

FINEST MIXED PETUNIAS.
A very rich mixture; composed of a great variety of brilliant colors, a superb strain for any garden.
Pkt. 10 cts.; ¼ oz. 40 cts.; oz. $1.50.

Mixed. A mixture of good sorts, pkt. 5 cts.; ¼ oz. 20 cts., oz. 75 cts.

PHLOX DRUMMONDII. One of our most useful and beautiful garden plants, free-bloomers of very brilliant colors; splendid for beds, borders or edgings. *Hardy Annual.* 1 to 1½ ft.

LARGE-FLOWERING PHLOX DRUMMONDII.
A magnificent mixture of the large-flowering or *Grandiflora* class; flowers as large as those of Perennial Phloxes. The richest variety of colors yet produced in the annual varieties. Remain in bloom during the entire season and are most beautiful and effective.
Pkt. 10 cts.; 3 pkts. for 25 cts.; ¼ oz. 30 cts.; oz. $1.00.

Choice Mixed. Finest mixture of all sorts, pkt. 5 cts.; oz. 75 cts.

Cuspidata, Finest Mixed (*New Star Phloxes*). Charming class with showy flowers, especially good for bouquets, pkt. 10 cts.; 3 pkts. 25 cts.; ¼ oz. 40 cts.; oz. $1.50.

Fimbriata, Finest Mixed. A choice mixture of the very best fringed varieties, pkt. 10 cts.; 3 pkts. 25 cts.; ¼ oz. 40 cts.; oz. $1.50.

Nana Compacta, Finest Mixed. A very dwarf-growing and really handsome class, ½ ft., pkt. 10 cts.

Perennial Phlox, Mixed (*Decussata*). Perfectly hardy tall-growing plants, bearing immense trusses of beautiful flowers of rich and varied colors, 3 ft., pkt. 10 cts.

POPPIES. For brilliancy and grand effect the poppy stands unrivalled; the improved varieties are certainly splendid and we cannot say too much in their favor. *Annuals* except as noted 1 to 2 ft.

GOLDEN GATE POPPIES.
Recall to mind every color you have ever seen in Poppies, then imagine every conceivable combination of colors—striped, blotched, edged, and bordered —on both single, semi-double, and double flowers, and you will have but a faint idea of the wondrously varied beauty of the new Golden Gate Poppies. No sight the past summer excited more attention nor called forth more expressions of wonder and amazement than our large block of these Poppies,—with thousands of open flowers of which seemingly there were no two alike.
Pkt. 10 cts.; 3 pkts. for 25 cts.

Danebrog. Brilliant single scarlet poppy, blotched with silvery white, a fine sort, pkt. 5 cts.

The Shirley Poppy. Large and elegant flowers; a very rich and effective mixture; noted for their beautiful light shades of white and pink; very desirable, pkt. 10 cts.; 3 pkts. for 25 cts.

Umbrosum. Glowing vermilion, with a deep black spot on each petal; very showy, pkt. 5 cts.

Mikado. New, fringed white flowers with purple margin; a choice sort, pkt. 10 cts.; 3 pkts. for 25 cts.

Mixed Annual Varieties. A very rich mixture of the best varieties; scatter the seed liberally in the garden and a mass of beauty will result, pkt. 5 cts.; oz. 40 cts.

Iceland or Perennial Poppies. Perfectly hardy and in bloom from June until frost; beautiful crushed, satin-like flowers of every color, pkt. 10 cts.; 3 pkts. for 25 cts.

Orientale. The darkest red *perennial* poppy; perfectly hardy, magnificent sort, 3 ft., pkt. 10 cts.; 3 pkts. for 25 cts.

PORTULACA. Nothing need be said about the cultivation of the portulaca as they do well anywhere; our assortments include the very newest and best colors. *Hardy Annual.* ½ ft.

ROSE-FLOWERED PORTULACAS.
From this mixture, more than one-half of the plants will produce magnificent double flowers; these can be transplanted eight inches apart as soon as they bloom, thus making the entire bed of double flowers. Unsurpassed for rich and brilliant colors; contains all the best double varieties.
Pkt. 10 cts.

Extra Single Mixed. A most elegant mixture; flowers large and of every shade of color, pkt. 5 cts.; oz. 50 cts.

PRIMULA (*Chinese Primrose*). One of our most beautiful and indispensable plants for winter blooming in the house or conservatory. The ease with which Primroses can be grown from seed makes them a very popular window plant. *Greenhouse Perennial.* ¾ ft.

Superb Mixture. An elegant mixture, embracing all the best large-flowered varieties, pkt. 50 cts.

PYRETHRUM. A pretty dwarf border plant, very largely used for edgings. *Perennial.* ¾ ft.

Parthenifolium Aureum (*Golden Feather*). Golden foliage, a splendid bedding plant, pkt. 10 cts.; oz. $1.00.

RHODANTHE, Mixed. Handsome everlasting flowers. *Hardy Annual.* 1 ft., pkt. 5 cts.

RICINUS (*Castor-Oil Bean*). One of our best ornamental-leaved plants, largely used for the center of beds; large palm-like leaves. Very easily grown from seed. *Half-hardy Annual.*

Borboniensis. Dark green foliage, a noble plant. 15 ft., pkt. 5 cts.; oz. 25 cts.

Sanguineus. Blood-red foliage and fruit. 7 ft., pkt. 5 cts.; oz. 25 cts.

SALPIGLOSSIS (*Velvet Flower*). A very ornamental and useful border plant with large mottled and veined petunia-like flowers. *Half-hardy Annual.* 1½ ft.

Large Flowering Mixed. Beautiful richly colored flowers; a splendid strain, pkt. 10 cts.

SALVIA. One of our most showy summer flowering plants, forming compact bushes, which are literally ablaze with brilliant flowers; very easily raised from seed, blooming the first season. *Perennials.*

Patens. Sky-blue, beautiful, 2½ ft., pkt. 25 cts.

SALVIA SPLENDENS.
LARGE-FLOWERING SCARLET SAGE.
Brilliant scarlet, one of the finest plants that ever grew in any garden; will remain for months a perfect blaze of color. Very easily grown from seed; blooming all through the summer and autumn. No garden is complete without it—a splendid plant, 2½ ft.
Pkt. 10 cts.; ¼ oz. 60 cts.

SCABIOSA (*Mourning Bride*). An old flower but deserving a place in every garden; as its rich and beautiful colors, as well as its profuse blooming, make it very useful. Also excellent for cut flowers. *Hardy Annual.*

Finest Double Mixed. Large, double flowers of splendid colors, 2 ft., pkt. 5 cts.; oz. 60 cts.

Dwarf Double Mixed. A very choice mixture of the dwarf sorts, 1 ft., pkt. 5 cts.; oz. 50 cts.

SCHIZANTHUS, Mixed. *Annual Sorts.* 1 ft., pkt. 5 cts.

SENSITIVE PLANT. Pinkish-white. *Annual.* 1½ ft., pkt. 5 cts.

SILENE (*Catch-fly*). **Finest Mixed.** *Annual.* 1 ft., pkt. 5 cts.

SMILAX. The popular climber. *Tender Perennial.* 10 ft., pkt. 10 cts.; oz. $1.00.

SOLANUM, Finest Mixed. *Tender Perennial.* 1½ ft., pkt. 10 cts.

STOCKS (*Gilliflowers*). These well-known favorites require no description; equally good as garden or house plants; our collection is composed of the very choicest dwarf sorts. *Half-hardy Annual.* 1 ft.

Largest-Flowering German Ten-Weeks Stocks. Our special strain of this splendid double-flowering variety is unsurpassed and will give the best of satisfaction wherever grown, height about 1 ft. and plants very compact; we offer the following colors:—
White—Crimson—Canary Yellow—Rose—Violet—Carmine—Dark Red. Each color separate, per pkt. 15 cts.

LARGEST-FLOWERING STOCKS. A superb mixture of the splendid colors just described, together with some twenty-five other elegant shades. These *large-flowering German Ten-Weeks Stocks* are the very best for garden or pot-culture; being richly fragrant and of the most brilliant colors. **Pkt. 15 cts.; 2 pkts. for 25 cts.; or 10 pkts. for $1.00; ¼ oz. $1.25; oz. $4.00.**

SWEET PEAS. From year to year the named varieties of sweet peas in cultivation are being constantly increased; until it has become practically impossible to make a satisfactory selection, from the almost endless number of varieties offered. I had in my trial grounds this past season every variety of sweet pea that I thought would prove to be of value; and from my trials I have condensed a long list of over one hundred kinds, to the following "selected varieties" which I can recommend as first-class in every respect. *Please see specialty pages in the first part of this catalogue; for full description of my now famous assortment "Faxon's Boston Mixture"* and also for cultivation notes of this splendid hardy annual. 6 ft.

Faxon's "Boston Mixture" Sweet Peas. The best mixture it is possible to offer; includes all varieties, both new and old, that produce flowers of the largest size and most splendid colors. *See specialty pages in first part of this catalogue for full description.*
Pkt. 5 cts.; oz. 15 cts.; ¼ lb. 50 cts.; lb. $1.50.

TWENTY-FIVE SELECTED VARIETIES.

☞ALL THESE SWEET PEAS ARE 5 cents per packet; 15 cents per ounce; 50 cents per ¼ pound; $1.50 per pound.

America. The brightest blood-red striped.
Blanche Burpee. The largest white.
Celestial. Clear lavender blue.
Crown Jewel. Creamy white veined violet rose.
Countess of Radnor. Pale mauve or lavender.
Duke of Clarence. Rosy claret.
Emily Eckford. Heliotrope.
Firefly. Fiery scarlet.
Gray Friar. Blue-gray.
Her Majesty. Soft, rosy pink.
Invincible Carmine. Shining crimson-scarlet.
Katherine Tracy. Brilliant pink.
Lady Penzance. Bright orange pink.
Lemon Queen. Blush pink and lemon.
Lottie Eckford. Lavender-shaded heliotrope.
Meteor. Rich orange salmon.
Miss Blanche Ferry. Large, pink and white. An improved *Painted Lady.*
Mrs. Eckford. Delicate primrose.
Mrs. Jos. Chamberlain. White ground striped with bright rose.
Princess Beatrice. Blush pink, marked with deeper shades.
Princess of Wales. White, striped lavender and mauve.
Ramona. Creamy white flaked with soft pink.
Splendour. Bright rose, flushed with crimson.
Stanley. Deep maroon.
Venus. Salmon buff.
(*See "Faxon's Specialties" also.*)

SWEET WILLIAM (*Dianthus Barbatus*). The favorite hardy border plants, with beautiful large heads of bloom of many colors; fine as cut flowers. *Hardy Biennial.* 1½ ft.
Double Mixed. A very choice mixture, pkt. 10 cts.; oz. $1.00.
Single Mixed. An assortment of all the most brilliant colors, pkt. 5 cts.; oz. 40 cts.
(*See also Carnations and Dianthus.*)

THUNBERGIA (*Black-Eyed Susan*). Pretty, slender-growing climber, rapidly covering wire trellises, and also useful for vases in the garden or house. *Half-hardy Annual.* 5 ft.
Finest Mixed. Many pretty colors, pkt. 5 cts.

VERBENA. If it were possible it seems to us that verbenas are becoming more popular every year; the plants thrive in any good garden soil, *and if grown from seed are more vigorous than if started from cuttings.* Our mixtures are very carefully selected and include all the best varieties. 1½ ft.

SUPERB MAMMOTH VERBENAS. My seed is saved from an elegant collection of named varieties, and produces very large flowers of the richest and most brilliant colors; this, my best mixture, will produce healthy plants, that will bloom most profusely from early summer until late autumn;—either in the garden or as pot-plants.
Pkt. 15 cts.; 2 pkts. for 25 cts.; ¼ oz. 85 cts.; oz. $3.00.

Fine Mixed. A good mixture, pkt. 5 cts.; oz. $1.50.

VIOLET (*Viola*). These fragrant flowers are easily grown from seed and will bloom most abundantly in a cool, moist situation. *Hardy Perennial.* ½ ft.
Finest Mixed. Best fragrant sorts, pkt. 10 cts.

VISCARIA, Mixed. *Annual.* 1 ft., pkt. 5 cts.

WALLFLOWER. Well-known plants, with large spikes of deliciously fragrant flowers and beautiful, deep colors. *Half-hardy Perennial.* 1½ ft.
Finest Mixed Branching. Best double varieties, pkt. 15 cts.

WHITLAVIA, Mixed. *Annual.* 1 ft., pkt. 5 cts.

ZINNIAS. One of our most stately and showy border plants, a strong grower and therefore succeeds well even if the ground is not very rich, but ample cultivation will be well repaid. Excellent for cut flowers and in the garden they bloom continually. *Hardy Annual.*

BEST DOUBLE ZINNIAS. My very best mixture; large, double flowers, that are unsurpassed for brilliancy and richness. The plants are very robust and clothed with luxuriant foliage; bloom the entire season and are splendid as cut-flowers, besides their great value in the flower garden, 2 ft.
Pkt. 10 cts.; 3 pkts. for 25 cts.; oz. $1.00.

I also offer the following separate colors of my **Best Double Zinnias,** *White—Sulphur Yellow—Golden Yellow—Flesh Color—Rose—Lilac—Scarlet—Crimson—Purple—Dark Purple.* Each color separate, per pkt. 10 cts.; any 3 pkts. for 25 cts., or the entire collection of 10 pkts. for 75 cts.

Curled and Crested. A fine strain of very choice colors, with curled and twisted petals, 2½ ft., pkt. 10 cts.

Dwarf Double Mixed. A superb mixture of the dwarfer growing varieties, fine for borders or pot-culture, ¾ ft., pkt. 10 cts.; oz. $1.00.

ORNAMENTAL GRASSES. Much used for ornamental gardening and borders, also nice when dried for winter bouquets. *Hardy Annuals* except as noted.
Animated Oats (*Avena Sterilis*). 2½ ft., pkt. 5 cts.
Feather Grass (*Stipa Pennata*). *Hardy Perennial.* 1½ ft., pkt. 5 cts.
Job's Tears (*Coix Lachryma*). 2 ft., pkt. 5 cts.
Love Grass (*Eragrostis Elegans*). 1½ ft., pkt. 5 cts.
Quaking Grass (*Briza Maxima*). 1 ft., pkt. 5 cts.
Mixture of Ornamental Grasses. 1 to 3 ft., pkt. 5 cts.; oz. 40 cts.

Faxon's $1 Collection of House Plants.

This unusual offer is made to meet, an almost daily demand for decorative and flowering plants for the "Window Garden." **This unequalled collection comprises the following seven elegant plants;** all of which are most easily cared for and very decorative.

ARECA LUTESCENS.—(Golden Stem Palm). One of the most beautiful palms in cultivation.

LATANIA BORBONICA—(Chinese Fan Palm). This popular variety is too-well known to require description. (*See illustration.*)

OTAHEITE ORANGE—The best of the Oranges for house-culture.

CYRTOMIUM FALCATUM—(Holly Fern). One of the most desirable Ferns for house-culture.

ASPARAGUS PLUMOSUS NANUS—(Asparagus Fern). This is a most effective decorative plant.

CYPERUS ALTERNIFOLIUS—(Umbrella Plant). An excellent pot-plant; thrives in any good soil.

SANSEVIERA ZEALANICA — An elegant variegated plant, especially adapted for house-culture; the thick leathery leaves standing the heat and dust of the house with impunity.

CHINESE FAN PALM.

For One Dollar I will send you **one good, strong plant** of each of the above seven elegant varieties for $1.00, by mail, postpaid.

☞ **These seven elegant plants** purchased separately would cost you several times the price charged; and it is only by selling large quantities that we are able to mail you this collection for $1.00. *Therefore please remember that we cannot make any changes whatever in this collection.* **We can mail you "Faxon's $1 Collection of House Plants" any day in the year.** ☜

Faxon's $1 Collection of Hardy Water Lilies.

No plants have acquired such universal appreciation within so short a period as Aquatics. The hardy varieties may be planted as soon as vegetation commences in the Spring. If not convenient to cultivate them in a pond or lily tank, they may be easily grown in tubs, several varieties being well adapted to this mode of culture. The tubs may be plunged in the ground or stand on the level, as the grower may determine. Fill the tubs two-thirds full of turfy soil enriched with decomposed hot-bed or farmyard manure; cow manure is very desirable; cover with two inches of sand and fill with water. The crowns of the plants should be placed just under the surface of the soil.

HARDY WATER LILIES.

For One Dollar I will send you **Three Elegant Hardy Water Lilies**—(one pink, one white, and one yellow) for $1.00, by mail, postpaid.

☞ These three Elegant Hardy Water Lilies will make a most splendid display either in a tub of water (see illustration), pond or other situation where they can have sunshine, water and rich soil. ☜

SUMMER FLOWERING BULBS.

GLADIOLUS—OUR SUPERB MIXTURE. 5 cents each; 50 cents per dozen; $3.00 per hundred.
If desired by mail add 10 cents per dozen for postage.

LILIES.

AURATUM (*The Golden-Rayed Lily of Japan*). 25 cents each; $2.50 per dozen.

SPECIOSUM (*Japan*) **ALBUM.** 30 cts. each; $3 doz.
" " **RUBRUM OR ROSEUM.** 20 cts. each; $2.00 doz.
If desired by mail add 5 cents per bulb for postage.

BEGONIAS (Tuberous-Rooted).

SINGLE-FLOWERED—SPLENDID MIXTURE OF COLORS. 10 cents each; $1.00 per dozen; by mail, postage paid.

DOUBLE-FLOWERED — SPLENDID MIXTURE OF COLORS. 25 cents each; $2.50 per dozen; by mail, postage paid.

DAHLIAS.

SHOW VARIETIES AND POMPON VARIETIES —SPLENDID ASSORTMENT. 20 cents each; $2.00 per dozen.
If desired by mail add 5 cents per bulb for postage.

TUBEROSES—DWARF EXCELSIOR PEARL. 5 cents each; 40 cents per dozen; $2.00 per hundred.
If desired by mail add 15 cents per dozen for postage.

MADEIRA VINES. 5 cents each; 50 cents per dozen.
If desired by mail add 10 cents per dozen for postage.

CALADIUM ESCULENTUM (*Elephant's Ear*). 20 cents each; $2.00 per dozen.
If desired by mail add 5 cents per bulb for postage.

CANNAS—BEST ASSORTED DWARF FRENCH CANNAS. 20 cents each; $2.00 per dozen.
If desired by mail add 5 cents per bulb for postage.

GLOXINIAS—BEST MIXTURE. 20 cts. each; $2.00 per doz.
If desired by mail add 15 cents per dozen for postage.

"FAXON'S HARVARD LAWN GRASS SEED."

Per pint, 15 cents; quart, 25 cents; half-peck, 65 cents; peck, $1.00; bushel, $4.00.
If by mail, add 5 cents per quart for postage.

☞ Also Timothy, Red Top, Orchard, Kentucky Blue, and all Grasses and Clovers always in stock—prices on application.

FERTILIZERS OF ALL KINDS.

PURE SHEEP MANURE—splendid for Lawns and all purposes, $2.50 per 100 lbs.

OUR NEW SWEET CORN,
THE FAXON.

It gives us great pleasure to be able to offer our customers, seed of so excellent and superior a vegetable as "The Faxon" Sweet Corn. **This is its first appearance and we have attained so near perfection in this, our latest introduction, that we have named it "The Faxon" Sweet Corn.** We send out this new variety as one of the very best early sorts known. It is a cross of the "Crosby's Early" with one of the best later varieties and possesses more excellence than any variety of sweet corn we have ever grown. Generally it possesses the character of the Crosby, having the same excellent flavor, with a larger and finer looking ear; the cob has a tinge of pink while the kernel, when in cooking condition is as clean and white as a hound's tooth. **It is earlier than "Crosby's Early," and grows a third taller, giving more ears to the stock and supplying an abundance of fodder.** The kernels are set evenly and regular in straight rows the entire length of the cob, and the ears fill out even over the "tips." Its appearance when ready for market is something beautiful and growers will find that "The Faxon" Sweet Corn "will take" in all markets; in short, for earliness, vigor of growth, productiveness, and handsome appearance, also for quality when cooked in green state, we believe it unequalled by any variety now known. We have but a very limited quantity to offer this season and would urge intending purchasers to order early if they wish to secure seed. **PER PACKET 20 CENTS; 6 PACKETS FOR $1.00.**

THE COMING NEW CUCUMBER.

Livingston's
Emerald.

A Dark Green Cucumber That Will Hold Its Color.

LIVINGSTON'S EMERALD retains every good point in the best strains of White Spine, and, in addition possesses that rich, dark green color which has been so long sought for but never before obtained. **It is strictly an evergreen, retaining its color until fully ripe.** On sight, its distinct dark green and spineless skin attracts the attention of everyone interested. The fruit sets early, and its vigorous vines abound in long, straight, handsome fruits of the most desirable qualities. **As a slicer the flesh is peculiarly crisp and tender, and the flavor most pleasing.** The young fruit being dark green, straight and tender, makes an excellent pickle, and when ripe none excels it for making sweet pickles. **For growing under glass it is most highly recommended.**

PKT. 10 CTS.; 3 PKTS. FOR 25 CTS.

"THE FAXON" SWEET CORN.

"FAXON'S EARLY BOSTON" CAULIFLOWER.

FAXON'S EARLY BOSTON
CAULIFLOWER.

FAXON'S SPECIALTIES.

We have given a great deal of attention to securing an extra early, sure heading cauliflower, and after many exhaustive trials can confidently say that this sort, whether intended for private use, or to be grown for market, is equal if not superior to any variety ever offered. For forcing under glass during winter and early spring, or for planting later in the open ground, no variety can surpass it. **In fact its earliness, dwarf, compact habit, and producing, as it does, large snow-white heads,** has made this cauliflower a great favorite with all who have given it a trial. Our seed this season is the product of the very finest specimens, and cannot fail to give every satisfaction.

Per packet, 25 cts.; ¼ ounce, $1.00; ounce, $4.00; ¼ pound, $14.00.

Boston's Best Cabbage.

IMPROVED STONE-MASON CABBAGES.

The Improved STONE=MASON Cabbage.

This famous variety has always been the favorite cabbage of the Boston market. For a great many years it has been grown both by market gardeners and private growers almost to the exclusion of all other sorts; and no main crop variety has ever been found to take its place. The heads are deep, round, of medium size, and very hard and solid; the outer leaves wrapping over the head very closely and handsomely. It is always sure to head — no sort surpasses it in this respect. As the heads are very thick through, so very solid and nearly round, it makes a most excellent sort to carry through the winter. **This cabbage has been so carefully trained and selected for so many years by some of the most noted cabbage growers in New England, that the present type is as near perfection as it is possible to obtain.** Being such a splendid keeper it is unsurpassed for shipping purposes, and is a most excellent sort for retailing or to sell by the barrel, being so very heavy and of such fine quality. Every kitchen garden should contain this cabbage, as its many splendid qualities make it one of the very best fall and winter vegetables. My seed is direct from the originator, and I know will give perfect satisfaction.

Per pkt. 10 cts.; oz. 40 cts.; lb. $4.00.

NEW ROCKY FORD MELON.

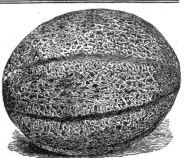

NEW ROCKY FORD MELON.

This delicious cantaloupe melon has been grown on a very large scale, and to a wonderful degree of perfection, in Rocky Ford, Colorado. From that section it has been shipped to every city in the country, and sold in the markets under the name of the town from which it came. **In fact, it seems to have "taken the country by storm"; many of our larger and well-known cantaloupes being passed by to give the preference to the sweeter and now famous "Rocky Ford Melons" from Colorado.** It is by far the most popular sort on the market, and commands higher prices than any other variety. The true type is shown by our illustration, the shape being oval and the average length about five inches. It is very sweet and most delicately flavored, with exceedingly fine and smooth-grained flesh of a light green color.

Per pkt. 10 cts.; oz. 20 cts.; lb. $2.00.

27

"The True" Danvers Carrot.

FAXON'S SPECIALTIES. This variety originated in Danvers, Mass., where the raising of carrots is made a special business, twenty to thirty tons per acre being no unusual crop. **It is now grown largely everywhere on account of its great productiveness and adaptability to all classes of soils.** Tops medium size, roots deep orange, large but medium length, tapering uniformly to a blunt point. Smooth and. handsome flesh, sweet, crisp and tender. Although of medium length it gives the largest yield per acre of any carrot. The best carrot for the market gardener or family use.

Per pkt. 5 cts.; oz. 15 cts.; lb. $1.50.

SAVOY CABBAGE. "Quincy Market."

FAXON'S SPECIALTIES. This selected strain of the true Boston type of this favorite cabbage will, we are sure, be found the equal, if not superior of any offered. Its dwarf habit, good size, and solid heading qualities will be appreciated by market gardeners who have experienced trouble in getting first-class stocks of Globe Curled Savoy Cabbage. This sort is unquestionably the finest flavored cabbage that has ever been brought to this market. Those who have never grown Savoy Cabbages in the home garden have a rich treat in store for them if they will plant this sort. Per pkt. 10 cts.; oz. 40 cts.; lb. $4.00.

"THE TRUE" DANVERS CARROT.

QUINCY MARKET SAVOY CABBAGE.

DANVERS ONION. "True Yellow Globe."

FAXON'S SPECIALTIES. Our Stock of Onion Seed is raised with particular care, none but the very best and earliest onions being selected for seed stock. Exercising such care, we claim for it a quality superior to most of that in the market. We have again harvested very large crops. **THE SEED IS PLUMP and HEAVY and of STRONG VITALITY, and we do not hesitate to recommend every ounce of our seed as thoroughly reliable in every respect.** Our old customers need no assurance as to the quality of our Onion Seed. To new customers we say " Give Our Seed a Trial."

PRICES
Per pkt. 5 cts.; oz. 20 cts.; ¼ lb. 60 cts.; lb.$2.00.

TRUE YELLOW GLOBE DANVERS ONION.

COPYRIGHT 1888.

BY M.B. FAXON.

In Massachusetts and especially in Essex County, the Danvers Onion has always been the standard sort grown, and the care and attention that has been given this vegetable has resulted in making our State famous the country over for its yellow onions. **Probably no gardeners in the world are more exacting and critical in regard to seed stocks than the growers of the Danvers Onion in Danvers and Peabody, Mass., the home of this vegetable;** no one who has not been in these towns and carefully examined this crop can have any adequate idea of what long and constant selection of the most perfect types for seed purposes has accomplished. Our strain is of good size, an early and abundant cropper, very thick bulb, flat or slightly convex bottom, full oval top, with small neck, and rich brownish-yellow skin. Seed from this type is more sure to bottom well than when grown from onions having too much depth of bulb or globe-shaped. These tend to stray into thick necks or scullions. We have taken the greatest care in selecting our seed stock for many years, and can fully recommend our strain to market gardeners and private growers as the finest in cultivation.

28

Burpee's Surehead Cabbage.

This cabbage produces large, round, flattened heads, of the Flat Dutch type, and is remarkable for its certainty to head. **It is all head, and always sure to head, even where other varieties fail.** The heads are remarkably uniform, very hard, firm, and fine in texture, and ordinarily weigh from ten to fifteen pounds each. It is very sweet flavored, has scarcely any loose leaves, keeps well, is good for shipping, and is just the variety and quality to suit market gardeners, farmers, and all lovers of good cabbage.

Per pkt. 10 cts.; oz. 30 cts.; 2 ozs. 50 cts.; ¼ lb. 85 cts.; ½ lb. $1.50; per lb. $3.00.

CANTALOUPE MELON.

LONG ISLAND BEAUTY.

This superb new variety originated on Long Island, N. Y. It is of the Hackensack type, but possesses so many advantages over that popular variety that it is no doubt destined to supersede it. The flesh is green and of the very finest quality, and the skin is densely netted. In shape it resembles the Hackensack, but is slightly more ribbed and is decidedly the most attractive looking melon we have ever seen. **Besides being the finest in quality and the most beautiful in appearance, it is also the earliest of all. You will be pleased with this splendid Cantaloupe Melon.**

Pkt. 10 cts.; oz. 20 cts.; lb. $2.00.

CANTALOUPE MELON—LONG ISLAND BEAUTY.

SILVER GREENS.

These Greens are the most delicious vegetable that it is possible to imagine. To my taste they are superior to dandelions or spinach, and are much easier to grow than either. Plant the seed thinly in rows, and cultivate the same as you do beets. Silver Greens, or Swiss Chard Beet, has one very desirable quality which has made it so popular, and that is, that as soon as the tops are gathered (it is the tops of this beet that are used for greens), they will immediately spring up again, and keep growing the entire season without regard to the number of times they are cut down; on this account a small bed of this species will supply a large family. **I feel confident you will thank me for bringing this desirable vegetable to your notice.** The seed I offer was grown by an expert, and is of the best quality. One-quarter pound of this seed will plant a bed of sufficient size to supply a family of ten persons with greens the entire season. Taking this as a basis, you can easily tell how much seed you need.

Pkt. 5 cts.; oz. 10 cts.; ¼ lb. 30 cts.; lb. $1.00.

Thorburn's Mammoth Butter Lettuce.

This is a highly improved (*black-seeded*) strain of the old butter lettuce. It is the most popular with the large Market-Gardeners around New York and more of it is grown and sold here than of any other sort. **It produces very large solid heads and is remarkably heat-resisting—remaining a long time, even in very warm weather, without shooting up.** The outside is green, but it becomes more and more yellow towards the centre. The heads are very compact and therefore especially suitable for market, as they stand handling well. The quality is unsurpassed; and altogether it is a most desirable variety for the home garden.

Pkt. 10 cts.; oz. 25 cts.; lb. $2.50.

THORBURN'S MAMMOTH BUTTER LETTUCE.

Standard Vegetable Seeds

Under this heading are listed and described all the standard vegetables. From year to year I have discarded from my list, those varieties possessing little or no merit; **and retained none but proven reliable sorts**, which I am positive will meet the requirements of the most exacting gardener.

On all orders for flower or vegetable seeds in packets or ounces, the purchaser may select seeds to the value of **$1.25** for each one dollar sent me. Thus, anyone sending **$1.00** can select seeds in packets or ounces amounting to **$1.25**; for **$2.00**, seeds in packets or ounces to the value of **$2.50**, and so on. *This discount applies only to seeds IN PACKETS AND OUNCES.*

There are many varieties in the following list of such **UNQUESTIONED SUPERIORITY**, that no vegetable garden could be considered complete without them. That you may not overlook these vegetables when making up your orders—YOU WILL FIND THESE SORTS INCLOSED IN RULES, AND THUS DESIGNATED.

ARTICHOKE.

GREEN GLOBE. The best for general use, pkt. 10 cts.; oz. 30 cts.; lb. $3.00.

ASPARAGUS.

CONOVER'S COLOSSAL. A standard sort; very prolific and good quality, pkt. 5 cts.; oz. 10 cts.; lb. 50 cts.

ASPARAGUS ROOTS.

CONOVER'S COLOSSAL (*two years old*). Per hundred, $1.00.

BEANS—DWARF OR BUSH.

DWARF BEAN.
EARLY LONG YELLOW SIX WEEKS. The favorite green-podded string bean.
Pkt. 10 cts.; qt. 25 cts.; peck $1.25.

EARLY VALENTINE. Very early, round-podded, green string bean, pkt. 10 cts.; qt. 25 cts.; peck $1.25.
EARLY MOHAWK. Green, flat pods; a good market string bean, pkt. 10 cts.; qt. 25 cts.; peck $1.25.

DWARF BEAN.
GOLDEN WAX. The favorite, wax-podded, snap bean. Pkt. 10 cts.; qt. 30 cts.; peck $1.50.

BLACK WAX. Early, round yellow pods, tender snap bean, pkt. 10 cts.; qt. 30 cts.; peck $1.50.

DWARF HORTICULTURAL BEAN.
The favorite either for snap or shell beans; a splendid variety.
Pkt. 10 cts.; qt. 25 cts.; peck $1.25.

GODDARD, or BOSTON FAVORITE. Similar to the above but bears much larger pods and beans, pkt. 10 cts.; qt. 25 cts.; peck $1.25.
REFUGEE. A late sort, used for pickling; green pods, pkt. 10 cts.; qt. 25 cts.; peck $1.25.
WARDWELL'S KIDNEY WAX. One of our best wax-podded, string beans, pkt. 10 cts.; qt. 30 cts.; peck $1.50.

BURPEE'S BUSH LIMA BEAN.
Best dwarf Lima in cultivation; beans large and of most splendid quality.
Pkt. 10 cts.; qt. 40 cts.; peck $2.00.

BEANS.—POLE OR RUNNING.

POLE HORTICULTURAL BEAN.
The best bean for both string and shell.
Pkt. 10 cts.; qt. 30 cts.; peck $1.50.

RED CRANBERRY. Splendid string bean, very tender, pkt. 10 cts.; qt. 40 cts.; peck $2.00.
SCARLET RUNNER. Ornamental climber, scarlet flowers, pkt. 10 cts.; qt. 30 cts.; peck $1.75.

POLE BEAN.
INDIAN CHIEF. The best wax-podded snap bean. Pkt. 10 cts.; qt. 30 cts.; peck $1.50.

LARGE WHITE LIMA. The largest of the Limas; splendid quality, pkt. 10 cts.; qt. 40 cts ; peck $2.00.
SIEVA, OR SMALL LIMA. Splendid quality and productive, pkt. 10 cts.; qt. 40 cts.; peck $2.00.
DREER'S IMPROVED LIMA. Ripens early, and of good quality, pkt. 10 cts.; qt. 40 cts.; peck $2.00.

GARDEN BEETS.

EARLY ECLIPSE. Very early, dark red variety; good quality, pkt. 5 cts.; oz. 10 cts.; lb. 60 cts.
EGYPTIAN TURNIP BLOOD. One of the earliest, best when small; a fine sort, pkt. 5 cts.; oz. 10 cts.; lb. 60 cts.
EARLY BASTIAN. A quick growing, large red beet; flesh very tender, pkt. 5 cts.; oz. 10 cts.; lb. 60 cts.

EDMAND'S TURNIP BLOOD BEET.
A round, smooth, blood-red sort, splendid for main crop; either early or late.
Pkt. 5 cts.; oz. 10 cts.; lb. 60 cts.

DEWING'S TURNIP BLOOD. The old favorite variety for market or family use, pkt. 5 cts.; oz. 10 cts.; lb. 60 cts.
LONG SMOOTH BLOOD. Long, large, dark red sort, very prolific, pkt. 5 cts.; oz. 10 cts.; lb. 60 cts.

SWISS CHARD, OR SILVER BEET.
The leaves make delicious greens, should be grown by all.
Pkt. 5 cts.; oz. 10 cts.; ¼ lb. 30 cts.; lb. $1.00.

BEET FOR GREENS. Beet-top greens are easily grown, and very nice, pkt. 5 cts.; oz. 10 cts.; lb. 50 cts.

30

CATTLE BEETS.

MANGEL-WURZEL, NORBITON GIANT. Probably the best long red variety, oz. 10 cts.; lb. 40 cts.
MANGEL-WURZEL, GOLDEN TANKARD. Flesh deep yellow; a very heavy cropper, oz. 10 cts.; lb. 40 cents.
WHITE SILESIAN SUGAR BEET. Much used for feeding cattle, very nutritious, oz. 10 cts.; lb. 40 cts.

BORECOLE, OR KALE.

DWARF CURLED, OR GERMAN GREENS. Makes nice greens; easily grown, pkt. 5 cts.; oz. 10 cts.; lb. $1.00.
GREEN CURLED SCOTCH. A hardy variety, improved by frost, pkt. 5 cts.; oz. 10 cts.; lb. $1.00.

BROCCOLI.

PURPLE CAPE. Greenish-purple, cauliflower-like heads, pkt. 10 cts.; oz. 40 cts.; lb. $4.00.

BRUSSELS SPROUTS.

IMPROVED DWARF. Produces from the stem miniature heads resembling little cabbages; very delicious when cooked like cauliflower, pkt. 10 cts.; oz. 25 cts.; lb. $2.50.

CABBAGES.

EARLY JERSEY WAKEFIELD. A standard early variety, medium size, pyramidal-shaped heads, pkt. 5 cts.; oz. 30 cts.; lb. $3.00.

HENDERSON'S EARLY SUMMER CABBAGE.

The large, early summer sort, fine quality.
Pkt. 5 cts.; oz. 30 cts.; lb. $3.00.

FOTTLER'S BRUNSWICK. A sure-heading main crop cabbage of large size, pkt. 5 cts.; oz. 25 cts.; lb. $2.50.

Stone Mason Cabbage.

The favorite winter cabbage; sure to head and keeps well. Pkt. 5 cts.; oz. 30 cts.; lb. $3.00.

PREMIUM FLAT DUTCH. A standard sort much grown in the South, pkt. 5 cts.; oz. 20 cts.; lb. $2.00.

SAVOY CABBAGE.

"QUINCY MARKET." A special selected strain of this ever popular cabbage; leaves finely curled, heads compact and of the most delicious flavor. Equally desirable as a fall or winter variety. A splendid cabbage.
Pkt. 10 cts.; oz. 40 cts.; lb. $4.00.
(See "Faxon's Specialties" also.)

LARGE RED DRUMHEAD. The best red cabbage in cultivation; solid red heads, pkt. 5 cts.; oz. 30 cts.; lb. $3.00.

CARROTS.

EARLY SCARLET HORN. A half-long variety, early, and very desirable for family use, pkt. 5 cts.; oz. 10 cts.; lb. $1.00.

"TRUE" DANVERS CARROT.

Without question the best variety for general use; my strain is noted for its rich color and splendid keeping qualities. This sort is a large cropper and easily harvested.
Pkt. 5 cts.; oz. 15 cts.; lb. $1.50.
(See "Faxon's Specialties" also.)

LONG ORANGE. Long, large roots; very productive, good for table use or stock, pkt. 5 cts.; oz. 10 cts.; lb. 80 cts.

CAULIFLOWER.

"FAXON'S EARLY BOSTON." The best strain of cauliflower in cultivation; heads uniformly large, solid and compact. A great favorite with all who have given it a trial.
Pkt. 25 cts.; ¼ oz. $1.00; oz. $4.00; ¼ lb. $14.00.
(See "Faxon's Specialties" also.)

CELERY.

EARLY ARLINGTON. Tall growing variety, good for early use; fine flavor, pkt. 10 cts.; oz. 40 cts.; lb. $4.00.

GOLDEN SELF-BLANCHING CELERY.

A grand variety; solid, crisp, and of delicious flavor. Needs no banking-up; a good keeper and in every way most desirable.
Pkt. 10 cts.; oz. 40 cts.; lb. $4.00.

BOSTON MARKET. The favorite celery for winter use; solid, crisp and of best quality, pkt. 10 cts.; oz. 40 cts.; lb. $4.00.
HENDERSON'S WHITE PLUME. This sort needs very little earthing-up as it is naturally white, pkt. 10 cts.; oz. 30 cts.; lb. $3.00.

CORN.—SWEET OR SUGAR.

EARLY CORY. The earliest variety; kernels large, quality good, pkt. 10 cts.; qt. 25 cts.; peck $1.25.

SWEET CORN.

EARLY CROSBY. The standard early sweet corn; splendid quality.
Pkt. 10 cts.; qt. 25 cts.; peck $1.25.

MOORE'S CONCORD. A little later than Crosby with larger ears of fine quality, pkt. 10 cts.; qt. 25 cts.; peck $1.25.

SWEET CORN.

POTTER'S EXCELSIOR. A main crop corn; this is the sweetest sort in cultivation.
Pkt. 10 cts.; qt. 25 cts.; peck $1.25.

BLACK MEXICAN. Much prized as it is a deliciously sweet sort, medium early, pkt. 10 cts.; qt. 25 cts.; peck $1.25.

SWEET CORN.

STOWELL'S EVERGREEN. The standard main crop and late sweet corn, splendid quality.
Pkt. 10 cts.; qt. 25 cts.; peck $1.00.

SWEET CORN FOR FODDER. Makes the very best green feed for cattle, qt. 15 cts.; peck 75 cts.; bush. $2.50.

FIELD CORN.

LONGFELLOW. The standard yellow sort for main crop; long ears, large kernels and small cob, qt. 15 cts.; bush. $2.00.
MAMMOTH ENSILAGE. Very tall growing variety; produces an immense yield, bush. $2.00.

CRESS OR PEPPERGRASS.

CURLED CRESS. Makes a nice salad; especially when mixed with lettuce, has a warm, pungent taste, pkt. 5 cts.; oz. 10 cts.; lb. 80 cts.

WATER-CRESS.

WATER-CRESS. Makes a good salad in early spring, pkt. 10 cts.; oz. 40 cts.; lb. $4.50.

CUCUMBERS.

White Spine Cucumber.

The best variety, crisp, and of splendid flavor; largely grown for market.
Pkt. 5 cts.; oz. 10 cts.; lb. $1.00.

EARLY CLUSTER. A medium sized early sort, grows in clusters, pkt. 5 cts.; oz. 10 cts.; lb. 80 cts.

Long Green Cucumber.

One of the very best table sorts; very crisp, and a good yielder. Pkt. 5 cts.; oz. 10 cts.; lb. $1.00.

BOSTON PICKLING. The favorite variety for pickles; a splendid sort, pkt. 5 cts.; oz. 10 cts.; lb. $1.00.

DANDELION.

IMPROVED BROAD-LEAVED. Dandelion greens are liked by everyone; this is the best variety for home use or the market, pkt. 10 cts.; oz. 40 cts.; lb. $5.00.

EGG PLANT.

NEW YORK IMPROVED PURPLE. The best sort in cultivation, fruit large, and of delicious quality, pkt. 10 cts.; oz. 40 cts.; lb. $5.00.

ENDIVE.

GREEN CURLED. A splendid salad for fall and winter; this is the best variety, pkt. 5 cts.; oz. 25 cts.; lb. $2.50.

LEEK.

BROAD LONDON OR FLAG. A large variety, splendid for salads; the best for general use, pkt. 10 cts.; oz. 30 cts.; lb. $3.00.

LETTUCES.

DEFIANCE. One of our best head lettuces, solid and crisp; stands the summer heat well, pkt. 5 cts.; oz. 20 cts.; lb. $2.00.

Boston Curled Lettuce.
One of the best curled varieties; early, and of delicious quality.
       Pkt. 5 cts.; oz. 25 cts.; lb. $2.50.

HANSON. This sort is very popular as the large heads are solid and crisp, pkt. 5 cts.; oz. 20 cts.; lb. $2.00.

WHITE-SEEDED TENNIS-BALL. Grown exclusively under glass; a very fine firm heading sort, pkt. 10 cts.; oz. 40 cts.; lb. $4.00.

THE BEST "HEAD" LETTUCE.
"BLACK-SEEDED TENNIS-BALL." The best head lettuce in cultivation; crisp, tender, and of most delicious flavor.
       Pkt. 5 cts.; oz. 25 cts.; lb. $2.50.

MARTYNIA.

MARTYNIA PROBOSCIDEA. The best variety for pickles, pkt. 10 cts.; oz. 40 cts.; lb. $4.00.

Melons.—Musk or Cantaloupe.

BAY VIEW. Flesh light green; a large, fine flavored and productive melon, pkt. 5 cts.; oz. 10 cts.; lb. 80 cts.

Cantaloupe Melon.
THE HACKENSACK. Large, round, green-fleshed variety; very sweet and delicious.
       Pkt. 5 cts.; oz. 10 cts.; lb. $1.00.

MONTREAL GREEN NUTMEG. A very large, netted melon; fine quality, a popular sort, pkt. 5 cts.; oz. 10 cts.; lb. $1.00.

ARLINGTON NUTMEG MELON.
The favorite cantaloupe melon of the Boston market, splendid quality.
       Pkt. 5 cts.; oz. 10 cts.; lb. $1.00.

MELONS.—WATER.

PHINNEY'S EARLY WATERMELON.
An early, red-fleshed, oval sort; a splendid melon.
       Pkt. 5 cts.; oz. 10 cts.; lb. 80 cts.

COLORADO PRESERVING. A splendid preserving melon; very productive, flesh firm and solid, pkt. 5 cts.; oz. 10 cts.; lb. 80 cts.

MUSTARD.

WHITE or YELLOW. The young leaves make a nice salad, pkt. 5 cts.; oz. 10 cts.; lb. 30 cts.

MUSHROOMS.

ENGLISH SPAWN. We offer the very best and freshest spawn, sure to give satisfaction, lb. 15 cts.; 8 lbs. for $1.00.

ONIONS.

EARLY RED GLOBE. A fine-grained, early, red onion; of good size and mild flavor, pkt. 5 cts.; oz. 20 cts.; lb. $2.00.

WETHERSFIELD LARGE RED. The standard red sort, best for general crop, pkt. 5 cts.; oz. 20 cts.; lb. $2.00.

DANVERS ONION.
"TRUE YELLOW GLOBE." Boston has always been famous for its Danvers Onions; and my strain is the result of many years' most careful selection from the best types in this market. The Danvers Onion is the best yellow variety in cultivation; early, small neck, ripens evenly, and is a sure cropper.
       Pkt. 5 cts.; oz. 20 cts.; ¼ lb. 60 cts.; lb. $2.00.
(See "Faxon's Specialties" also.)

WHITE PORTUGAL. The favorite white onion; mild-flavored and productive, pkt. 10 cts.; oz. 30 cts.; lb. $3.00.

ONION SETS.

WHITE SETS. The best for general use; very mild-flavored, qt. 30 cts.; peck $1.75.

OKRA.

DWARF GREEN. Most productive, and very dwarf; a fine variety, pkt. 5 cts.; oz. 10 cts.; lb. $1.00.

PARSLEY.

CHAMPION MOSS CURLED. The favorite variety; elegantly curled and of a rich green color, pkt. 5 cts.; oz. 10 cts.; lb. $1.00.

PARSNIPS.
LONG SMOOTH WHITE. The standard variety; long, smooth, and productive.
       Pkt. 5 cts.; oz. 10 cts.; lb. 80 cts.

PEAS.

(As a help in ordering, I have stated the height of each variety.)

Earliest of All Peas.
The earliest variety, productive, and of good quality, 2½ ft.   Pkt. 10 cts.; qt. 25 cts.; peck $1.25.

EARLY DANIEL O'ROURKE. The favorite early pea, productive, and of good quality; 2½ ft., pkt. 10 cts.; qt. 25 cts.; peck $1.25.

MAUD S. Much liked, as it is very early and hardy, quality the best; 2½ ft., pkt. 10 cts.; qt. 25 cts.; peck $1.25.

BLISS' AMERICAN WONDER PEAS.
The sweetest, wrinkled, dwarf pea grown, perfectly delicious, 1 ft.
       Pkt. 10 cts.; qt. 30 cts.; peck $1.75.

BLISS' ABUNDANCE. Long, round, well-filled pods, sow thinly; 1½ ft., pkt. 10 cts.; qt. 25 cts.; peck $1.50.

BLISS' EVERBEARING. A very nice sort, large, full pods; very sweet; sow thinly; 2½ ft., pkt. 10 cts.; qt. 25 cts.; peck $1.25.

McLEAN'S ADVANCER PEAS.
The standard pea for market or garden, splendid quality, 2½ ft.
       Pkt. 10 cts.; qt. 25 cts.; peck $1.25.

YORKSHIRE HERO. An elegant pea, sow thinly as it is a spreading variety; 2½ ft., pkt. 10 cts.; qt. 25 cts.; peck $1.25.

STRATAGEM PEAS.

Very large pods and peas, splendid quality, a great favorite, 1½ ft.
Pkt. 10 cts.; qt. 30 cts.; peck $1.75.

HORSFORD'S MARKET GARDEN. A very prolific wrinkled pea of the best quality; 2½ ft., pkt. 10 cts.; qt. 25 cts.; peck $1.25.
CHAMPION OF ENGLAND. The popular tall growing wrinkled sort, delicious flavor; 5 ft., pkt. 10 cts.; qt. 25 cts.; peck $1.25.
BLACK-EYED MARROWFAT. The old, large marrow pea, much liked; 3 ft., pkt. 10 cts.; qt. 20 cts.; peck 75 cts.

PEPPERS.

LONG RED CAYENNE. Very pungent, bright red pepper; a productive sort, pkt. 5 cts.; oz. 30 cts.; lb. $3.00.
LARGE BELL, or BULL NOSE. An early, large pepper of milder flavor, much liked, pkt. 5 cts.; oz. 30 cts.; lb. $3.50.

SQUASH PEPPERS.

The standard sort, large, and very productive.
Pkt. 5 cts.; oz. 30 cts.; lb. $3.50.

POTATOES.

(Prices subject to variations of the market.)
BEAUTY OF HEBRON. One of the most popular early sorts in cultivation, bush. $2.00; bbl. $4.50.
EARLY ROSE. The reliable standard variety, bush. $2.00; bbl. $4.50.
SNOWFLAKE. Noted for its splendid quality, a fine variety, bush. $2.00, bbl. $4.50.

PUMPKINS.

CONNECTICUT FIELD. The standard variety to grow for stock; very productive, pkt. 5 cts.; oz. 10 cts.; lb. 40 cts.
SUGAR. A small fine-grained, sweet pumpkin; best sort for pies, pkt. 5 cts.; oz. 10 cts.; lb. 60 cts.

RADISHES.

EARLY SCARLET TURNIP. A very early, quick growing, round radish; fine flavor, pkt. 5 cts., oz. 10 cts.; lb. 80 cts.

FRENCH BREAKFAST RADISH.

The best short radish, scarlet with a white tip; delicious quality.
Pkt. 5 cts.; oz. 10 cts.; lb. 80 cts.

SCARLET TURNIP, WHITE TIPPED. Similar to first except the tip is white; a handsome sort, pkt. 5 cts., oz. 10 cts.; lb. 80 cts.

Long Scarlet Radish.

The best long variety either for forcing or the kitchen garden.
Pkt. 5 cts.; oz. 10 cts.; lb. 80 cts.

RHUBARB.

VICTORIA. The variety in general use, very productive, pkt. 5 cts.; oz. 25 cts.; lb. $2.50.

RHUBARB ROOTS.

VICTORIA. $2.00 Per Dozen.

SALSIFY.

LONG WHITE. Our strain is the mammoth variety and very choice, pkt. 5 cts.; oz. 15 cts.; lb. $1.50.

ROUND THICK-LEAVED SPINACH.

The standard spinach for early or late; of the best quality.
Pkt. 5 cts.; oz. 10 cts.; lb. 30 cts.

SQUASHES.

SUMMER CROOKNECK SQUASH.

The best summer squash, very large cropper; splendid quality.
Pkt. 5 cts.; oz. 10 cts.; lb. 80 cts.

WHITE BUSH SCALLOPED. The popular, flat summer sort, pkt. 5 cts.; oz. 10 cts.; lb. 80 cts.
BOSTON MARROW. The favorite summer and fall variety, pkt. 5 cts.; oz. 10 cts.; lb. 80 cts.

HUBBARD SQUASH.

The favorite sort for winter, of superior quality.
Pkt. 5 cts.; oz. 10 cts.; lb. 80 cts.

LOW'S BAY STATE. A splendid winter variety with hard blue shell; pkt. 5 cts.; oz. 10 cts.; lb. 80 cts.

Essex Hybrid Squash.

A splendid winter squash; shaped like the "American Turban"; but much superior, as it has a very hard shell.
Pkt. 5 cts.; oz. 10 cts.; lb. 80 cts.

CANADA CROOKNECK. The best of the winter Crooknecks, pkt. 5 cts.; oz. 10 cts.; lb. 80 cts.
MAMMOTH YELLOW. Very large, sometimes weighing two hundred pounds, pkt. 10 cts.; oz. 20 cts.; lb. $2.00.

TOMATOES.

Essex Hybrid Tomato.

I consider this sort the best tomato in cultivation for general use.
Pkt. 5 cts.; oz. 25 cts.; lb. $3.00.

LIVINGSTON'S BEAUTY. Large, smooth tomato; glossy-crimson with purplish tinge, flesh very solid and firm, pkt. 5 cts.; oz. 25 cts.; lb. $3.00.

Perfection Tomato.

A deep red, early variety; perfectly smooth and very productive.
Pkt. 5 cts.; oz. 25 cts.; lb. $3.00.

TURNIPS.

The Best Flat Turnip.

PURPLE TOP STRAP-LEAVED. The standard early, flat variety; equally good for winter use.
Pkt. 5 cts.; oz. 10 cts.; lb. 60 cts.

EXTRA EARLY MILAN. The earliest flat turnip, pkt. 5 cts.; oz. 10 cts.; lb. $1.00.

THE BEST YELLOW RUTA-BAGA.

CARTERS' IMPERIAL HARDY SWEDE. The standard yellow Swede or Ruta-Baga turnip.
Pkt. 5 cts.; oz. 10 cts.; lb. 60 cts.

WHITE EGG. An oval turnip of medium size; splendid quality, pkt. 5 cts.; oz. 10 cts.; lb. 60 cts.

Sweet German Turnip.

The standard white Swede; this is the famous Cape Cod turnip.
Pkt. 5 cts.; oz. 10 cts.; lb. 60 cts.

POT, SWEET, AND MEDICINAL HERBS.

CARAWAY. Pkt. 5 cts.; oz. 10 cts.; lb. 80 cts.
SWEET MARJORAM. Pkt. 5 cts.; oz. 25 cts.; lb. $2.50.
SAGE. Pkt. 5 cts.; oz. 20 cts.; lb. $2.50.
SUMMER SAVORY. Pkt. 5 cts.; oz. 20 cts.; lb. $1.75.
THYME. Pkt. 10 cts.; oz. 40 cts.; lb. $4.00.
WORMWOOD. Pkt. 10 cts.; oz. 30 cts.; lb. $3.00.

Mrs. Harrison.

" The beautiful Pansies which you sent arrived yesterday in good condition. I am exceedingly fond of Pansies, and never tire of looking at them and admiring the beautiful colors and different shades. Those you sent gave me much pleasure in admiring the size and color as I helped to place them in water."

Mrs. Cleveland.

"I was very glad to receive the Pansies which you were good enough to send me. They came in good condition, and were much enjoyed."

Mrs. McKinley.

" Mrs. McKinley requests me to thank you very sincerely for your gracious courtesy in sending her the flowers which she received in good condition."

THE BARTA PRESS, BOSTON.

CPSIA information can be obtained
at www.ICGtesting.com
Printed in the USA
BVHW040928141218
535629BV00022B/1051/P